LIVING REEFS
OF THE
INDO-PACIFIC
A PHOTOGRAPHIC GUIDE

LIVING REEFS
OF THE
INDO-PACIFIC
A PHOTOGRAPHIC GUIDE

Rob van der Loos

First published in Australia in 2001 by
Reed New Holland
an imprint of New Holland Publishers (Australia) Pty Ltd
Sydney • Auckland • London • Cape Town

14 Aquatic Drive, Frenchs Forest NSW 2086, Australia
218 Lake Road, Northcote, Auckland, New Zealand
Garfield House, 86 Edgware Road, London W2 2EA, United Kingdom
80 McKenzie Street, Cape Town 8001, South Africa

National Library of Australia Cataloguing-in-Publication Data:

Van der Loos, Rob.
Living Reefs of the Indo-Pacific : a photographic guide.

Includes index.
ISBN 1 876334 65 7.

1. Coral reef ecology - Indo-Pacific region. I. Title.

577.789

Publishing Manager: Louise Egerton
Commissioning Editor: Anouska Good
Project Editor: Rosemary Milburn
Editor: Anne Savage
Designer: Nanette Backhouse
Picture Researcher: Kirsti Wright
Production Controller: Wendy Hunt
Cartography: Guy Holt
Reproduction: DNL Resources Pty Ltd
Printer: Times Offset, Malaysia

Body copy is set in Latin 725 BT 9.5pt.

Picture on previous page: Dendronephthya Cowries (*Pseudosimnia punctata*) rasp away food particles
lodged within soft coral branches.

ACKNOWLEDGEMENTS

There is never just one person responsible for putting a book like this together. There are dive buddies who have helped in locating creatures, typists who have helped compile the information, editors who put all the information together into the final product, and of course there are the friends and family that give you the support to get over the finish line.

Very sincere thanks go to the following people who gave freely of their valuable time: Scott Michaels, Roger Steen, Dr Gerald Allen, Annemarie Köhler and Danja Köhler. A special thanks, too, to Marty Fenton for providing the series of photos on the *Rhinopious alphanes* shedding its skin shown on page 79. Thank you to Anouska Good for first taking the idea of the book and Rosemary Milburn and staff for the patience it took to put it together.

On a more personal note, to my family — Peo, Cherie, Malcolm, Jason, Maleta and Elvie — for the encouragement and help in researching and compiling the original draft, thank you.

This dying gorgonian is hosting many smaller hosts such as crinoids and *Dendronephthya* corals.

CONTENTS

INTRODUCTION

For many years now I have been involved in running cruises on a live-aboard dive boat, the M. V. *Chertan*, which is based in the Milne Bay waters of Papua New Guinea. During this time I have enjoyed the company of many professional and amateur underwater photographers. While most of them could certainly take fine pictures, many had no idea of just where to find the exotic creatures they dreamed of capturing on film. Asked for the ten-thousandth time, 'Where can I find this anemone/shrimp/coral?', I decided it was time to put down what knowledge I had accrued in a book, so here it is.

Many different habitats exist in the ocean realm — seagrass areas, pebble areas, rocky reefs, drop-offs, mud flats, sand flats and coral mounds. While many species range over a number of very different habitats, many others have evolved to suit the conditions of very specific ones. The major factors in the formation of any habitat are wave action, current and depth. Areas continuously pounded by wave action are usually unable to support the formation of hard corals but areas fed by strong currents tend to support huge varieties of fish life and soft corals. Increasing depth also tends to be reflected in changes in the characteristics of an area's inhabitants.

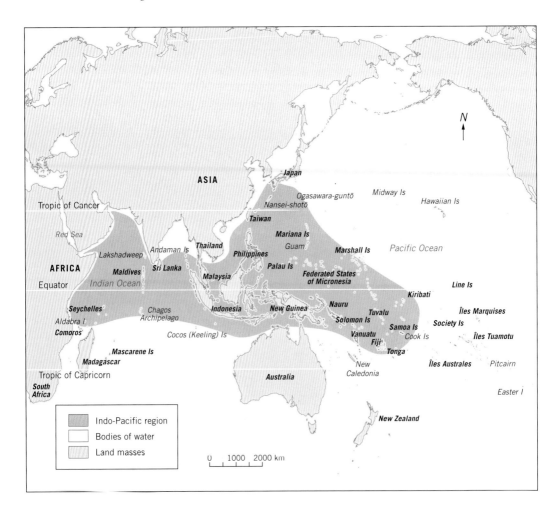

The smaller creatures of the reefs are often found within or upon larger organisms, either plants or animals. The relationships between these organisms can be quite one-sided, as in the case of the spindle cowries and soft corals. The cowries find shelter in the coral and use it as their food source, giving nothing in return. Other relationships are mutually beneficial, each creature relying on the other for its survival, like the shrimp goby and the blind shrimp. While the shrimp maintains the burrow that both need as protection against predators, the goby stands guard outside, warning of oncoming danger by slight movements of its tail.

The first chapter in this book looks at organisms that live closely with others. Some form specific relationships with just a single species, or several species from a single genus; others live among a broader spectrum of organisms.

Chapter 2 illustrates a few of the larger cowries commonly found in rubble areas, while Chapter 3 reveals the extraordinary beauty of some of the hundreds of sea slugs found in tropical waters.

Chapter 4 portrays several members of the dangerous scorpion-fish family. Before you dive in areas where these fish are found, make sure you know the location of the nearest medical centre with access to stocks of anti-venom for the Reef Stonefish and acquaint yourself with the appropriate first-aid techniques.

Chapter 5 illustrates the relationship that probably first springs to mind when one thinks of tropical reefs, that between sea anemones and the colourful anemonefish. Chapter 6 takes a different tack. Until recently, most people who dreamed of diving in tropical waters had only clear water and rich coral reefs in mind. While these areas remain the most popular dive sites, increasingly divers are looking to explore the habitats of the sandy, silty seaweed zone and the rubble (or muck) zone. The photographic bounty here is immense. Chapter 7 explores some techniques of underwater photography and discusses how to get the best effects.

The captions give each organism its common name (where it has one), its scientific name, a descriptive comment, and notes on depth, distribution and ideal lens for the subject. It was not my intent, however, to create a scientific identification manual, and I acknowledge that some of the scientific names may be open to correction. The depth suggests where you are most likely to find a particular creature. The first country listed under distribution is that where the photo was taken. (For organisms of whose scientific name I am uncertain I give only the country where the picture was taken.) The suggested ideal lens is simply my personal choice, the lens which I feel would best capture that particular creature. It also acts as a guide to relative size.

This book is purely and simply a field guide for locating some of the smaller inhabitants of the coral reefs of the Indo-Pacific. It has been compiled using the best information available at the time of writing, combined with 25 years of in-the-field experience gained over many thousands of dives. Whether you are a photographer or not, I hope you enjoy the result.

Rob van der Loos
Milne Bay, 2001

CHAPTER 1
LIVING HABITATS

This chapter is a guide to some of the associations between host organisms and smaller creatures in the Indo-Pacific region. Understanding relationships between creatures in the marine world makes it easier to find subjects to photograph. Animals such as hard and soft corals, sea stars (starfish), sea whips and sea fans (gorgonians) and crinoids (feather stars) host a multitude of tiny shellfish, shrimps, crabs and lobsters. In most cases the host derives no benefit from the relationship, merely — and inadvertently — providing shelter, and often food, to the other visitors. Even knowing which hosts to look for, however, you will still have to search carefully, as the small 'guests' are often well camouflaged and may mimic other forms. Many have the ability to change their colourings and patterning, sometimes within seconds. The marvels of such disguises are so ingenious they can take a diver's breath away, even after decades of exploring the reefs.

The crinoid shrimp *Periclimenes ceralophthalmus* feeds within the arms of the crinoid *Comantheria briareus*.
DEPTH RANGE: 10–400 m (33–125 ft).
DISTRIBUTION: PNG, Solomon Islands, Micronesia, Australia, Indonesia.
IDEAL LENS: 60–105 mm.

The crinoid shrimp *Periclimenes amboinensis* tends to adopt the colouration of its host, in this case the crinoid *Oxyconamthus bennetti*. (See also page 164.)
DEPTH RANGE: 4–15 m (12–50 ft).
DISTRIBUTION: PNG, Solomon Islands, Australia, Indonesia.
IDEAL LENS: 105 mm.

The Elegant Squat Lobster (*Allogalathea elegans*) associates with a variety of crinoids, sometimes taking on their colouring, although this is not always the case.
DEPTH RANGE: 5–20 m (15–65 ft).
DISTRIBUTION: PNG, throughout the Indo-Pacific.
IDEAL LENS: 105 mm.

The Crinoid Clingfish (*Discotrema* sp.) lives and feeds in and around crinoids. It, too, is able to take on the colour and patterning of its host, *Comanthina schegelii*.
DEPTH RANGE: 5–30 m (15–100 ft).
DISTRIBUTION: PNG, Solomon Islands, Australia, Indonesia.
IDEAL LENS: 105 mm

OPPOSITE: Crinoids, including this *Comanthina schegelii*, commonly host a variety of small marine creatures, such as fish, lobsters and shrimps. Clinging to hard surfaces, their feathery arms wave in the current.
DEPTH RANGE: 3–40 m+ (9–125 ft+). **DISTRIBUTION:** PNG, throughout the Indo-Pacific. **IDEAL LENS:** 15–60 mm.

The Black Spiral Coral (*Cirrhipathes spiralis*) harbours a variety of small creatures. Black corals have horny skeletons and so are not true corals. They have a single branch from which whip-like tentacles stretch to reach passing food. **DEPTH RANGE:** 3–40 m+ (9–125 ft+). **DISTRIBUTION:** PNG, throughout the Indo-Pacific. **IDEAL LENS:** 15 mm.

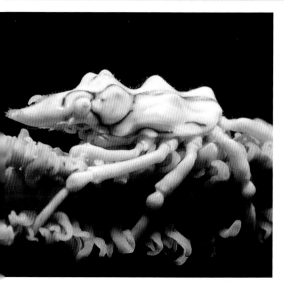

The bizarre little black coral crab *Xenocarcinus tuberculatus* clings to black-coral tentacles in strong current areas.
DEPTH RANGE: 5–40 m (15–125 ft).
DISTRIBUTION: PNG, Australia, Indonesia, Hong Kong, Taiwan, Japan, Red Sea, Philippines.
IDEAL LENS: 105 mm.

Hidden upon the waving tentacle of its black coral host, the tiny shrimp *Pontonides unciger* is easily overlooked by predators and photographers alike.
DEPTH RANGE: 5–40 m (15–125 ft).
DISTRIBUTION: PNG.
IDEAL LENS: 105 mm.

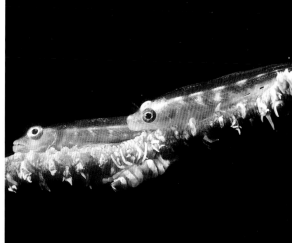

This black coral shrimp (*Pontonides* sp.) has yet to acquire a species name. It is most active when the polyps of the black coral are out feeding.
DEPTH RANGE: 5–10 m (15–35 ft), and possibly beyond.
DISTRIBUTION: PNG, Philippines, Hawaii.
IDEAL LENS: 105 mm.

These delicate, almost transparent, sea-whip gobies (*Bryaninops yongei*) 'stick' to surfaces by their pelvic fins, which are joined to form a sort of suction cup.
DEPTH RANGE: 3–40 m+ (9–125 ft+).
DISTRIBUTION: PNG.
IDEAL LENS: 105 mm.

This beautiful, spiky soft coral of the genus *Dendronephthya* is found on coral reefs and walls where there is a noticeable current. The various species of this genus play host to a number of small creatures, six of which appear opposite.
DEPTH RANGE: 4–40 m (12–125 ft). **DISTRIBUTION:** PNG, throughout the Indo-Pacific. **IDEAL LENS:** 15–35 mm.

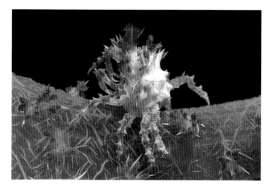

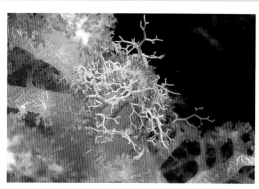

The Dendronephthya Crab (*Hoplophrys oatesii*) changes colour to blend in with its host. (See also page 163.)
DEPTH RANGE: 5–30 m (15–100 ft).
DISTRIBUTION: PNG, throughout the Indo-Pacific.
IDEAL LENS: 105 mm.

Ludwig's Basket Star (*Conocladus ludwigi*) emerges at night to feed among the polyps of soft corals.
DEPTH RANGE: 5–15 m (15–50 ft).
DISTRIBUTION: PNG, throughout the Indo-Pacific.
IDEAL LENS: 20–60 mm.

Dendronephthya Cowries (*Pseudosimnia punctata*) rasp away food particles lodged within soft coral branches.
DEPTH RANGE: 5–25 m (15–80 ft).
DISTRIBUTION: PNG, throughout the Indo-Pacific.
IDEAL LENS: 105 mm.

The brittle star *Ophiothrix purpurea* clambers about on many different hosts including the *Dendronephthya* corals.
DEPTH RANGE: 5–20 m (15–65 ft).
DISTRIBUTION: PNG, throughout the Indo-Pacific.
IDEAL LENS: 60 mm.

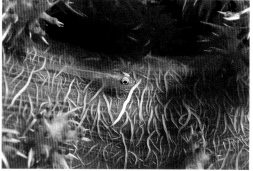

With a carapace less than 25 mm (1 in) long, the brilliantly-coloured porcelain crab (*Lissoporcellana* sp.) blends in with the spines of a *Dendronephthya* coral.
DEPTH RANGE: 5–20 m (15–65 ft).
DISTRIBUTION: PNG, Indonesia.
IDEAL LENS: 105 mm.

The aptly named Many-host Goby (*Pleurosicya mossambica*) frequents sponges, soft corals and sea cucumbers. Being almost transparent, it blends in with all its hosts.
DEPTH RANGE: 4–40 m (12–125 ft).
DISTRIBUTION: PNG, Solomon Islands, Australia, Indonesia.
IDEAL LENS: 105 mm.

This sea fan-like soft coral of the genus *Chironephthya* is found under ledges and in other places not receiving direct sunlight. It varies in colour from yellow–brown to blue, and hosts several animals. The polyps are quite widely separated.
DEPTH RANGE: 5–20 m (15–65 ft). **DISTRIBUTION:** PNG, throughout the Indo-Pacific. **IDEAL LENS:** 20–60 mm.

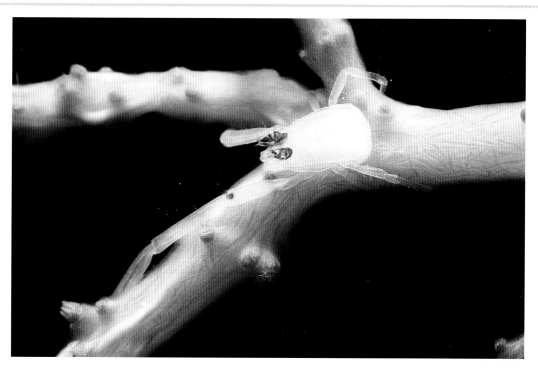

The Red-faced Squat Lobster (*Galathea* sp.) clambers along the branches of the *Chironephthya* soft coral. With its eyes mimicking the coral's retracted polyps and lying parallel to the branches, the lobster can be very difficult to spot.
DEPTH RANGE: 5–20 m (15–65 ft). **DISTRIBUTION:** PNG, throughout the Indo-Pacific. **IDEAL LENS:** 105 mm.

The black coral crab *Quadrella granulosa* is commonly found among the branches of *Chironephthya* soft corals, usually in pairs. It is also found on crinoids, sometimes in small colonies.
DEPTH RANGE: 5–15 m (15–50 ft). **DISTRIBUTION:** PNG, throughout the Indo-Pacific. **IDEAL LENS:** 105 mm.

This Mushroom Leather Coral, a species of *Sarcophyton*, occurs both as individuals and in large colonies in shallow reef areas and rubble bottoms. Besides providing a home for some small marine creatures, it is eaten by several sea snails and slugs.

DEPTH RANGE: 1–10 m (3–35 ft). **DISTRIBUTION:** PNG, throughout the Indo-Pacific. **IDEAL LENS:** 15–60 mm.

The quite bizarre nudibranch *Phyllodesmium longicirrum* is about 60 mm long. It is commonly found feeding on soft corals of the genus *Sarcophyton*. Once it has settled upon a food source, it may remain in the same position for months until the entire colony is consumed. (This nudibranch is also pictured on page 75.)
DEPTH RANGE: 5–25 m (15–80 ft).
DISTRIBUTION: PNG, throughout the Indo-Pacific.
IDEAL LENS: 15–60 mm.

The large white Egg Cowry (*Ovula ovum*) extrudes a jet black mantle. It feeds in shallow water on *Sarcophyton* soft corals.
DEPTH RANGE: 1–15 m (3–50 ft).
DISTRIBUTION: PNG, throughout the Indo-Pacific.
IDEAL LENS: 20 mm.

The Toenail Cowry (*Calpurnus verrucosus*) has a delicate spotted mantle. It, too, feeds on *Sarcophyton* soft corals.
DEPTH RANGE: 2–15 m (6–50 ft).
DISTRIBUTION: PNG, much of the Indo-Pacific.
IDEAL LENS: 60 mm.

Soft corals of the genus *Xenia* usually occur in colonies and are widespread throughout the Indo-Pacific. *Xenia* are poisonous to many fish but many species host some smaller creatures which are able to use their toxic polyps to their advantage.

DEPTH RANGE: 3 20 m (9–65 ft). **DISTRIBUTION:** PNG, throughout the Indo-Pacific. **IDEAL LENS:** 60–24 mm.

The Cardinal Fish (*Neamia octospina*) lurks among the waving branches of *Xenia*. Its closely-matching colouration makes it difficult for predators to spot.
DEPTH RANGE: 5–20 m (15–65 ft). **DISTRIBUTION:** PNG, Australia, Philippines. **IDEAL LENS:** 105 mm.

Hidden within a clump of poisonous *Xenia* polyps, the beautifully-camouflaged *Caphyra laevis* crab is safe from predators.
DEPTH RANGE: 5–20 m (15–65 ft). **DISTRIBUTION:** PNG, Australia, Philippines. **IDEAL LENS:** 105 mm.

Like the sea fans, soft corals are colonies of polyps housed within branched structures. They also feed in a similar way and host many small creatures. This sea fan, *Siphonogorgia godefroyi*, varies in colour from deep purple with white polyps to brown with light brown polyps.

DEPTH RANGE: 4–30 m (12–100 ft). **DISTRIBUTION:** PNG, Solomon Islands, Australia, Philippines. **IDEAL LENS:** 15 mm.

A close-up of the *Siphonogorgia* colony reveals a pair of browsing allied cowries (*Dentiovula dorsuosa*). These cowries range in colour from a very light purple-tinged white to a deep purple. They can be identified by a yellow–orange stripe on both ends and sometimes another stripe in the centre of the shell.

DEPTH RANGE: 4–30 m (12–100 ft).
DISTRIBUTION: PNG, Australia, Indonesia, Japan.
IDEAL LENS: 60 mm.

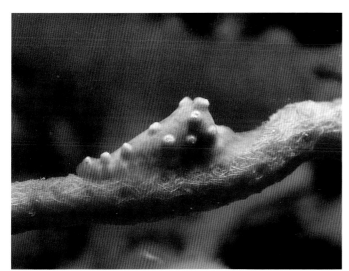

This unidentified allied cowry mimics the retracted tentacles of *Siphonogorgia godefroyi* polyps with its unusual knobbly mantle.

DEPTH RANGE: 3 m (9 ft).
DISTRIBUTION: PNG.
IDEAL LENS: 105 mm.

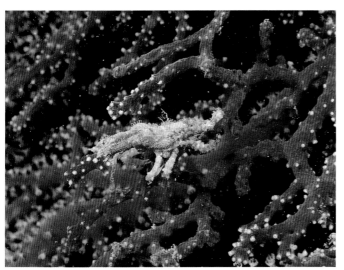

Spider crabs are masters of disguise. Their carapaces are studded with hooked hairs and spines upon which they drape bits of sponges, algae and hydroids to camouflage themselves. This Gorgonian Crab (*Xenocarcinus depressus*), has not quite matched its wardrobe with its *Siphonogorgia* host. (Another specimen of this species is pictured on page 41.)

DEPTH RANGE: 2–30 m (6–100 ft).
DISTRIBUTION: PNG, Australia, Indonesia.
IDEAL LENS: 105 mm.

The Blue Sea Star (*Linckia laevigata*) is a creature of both coral reefs and rubble bottoms. Organisms which use this sea star as a host are usually found on its underside. To photograph them you may have to be a little intrusive and turn the sea star over gently. Remember to turn the sea star back again when you have finished.

DEPTH RANGE: 0–6 m (0–20 ft). **DISTRIBUTION:** PNG, throughout the Indo-Pacific. **IDEAL LENS:** 20–60 mm.

Thyca crystallina is a small parasitic sea snail that lives and feeds on the underside of the Blue Sea Star, usually in shallow reef-top locations.
DEPTH RANGE: 0–6 m (0–20 ft). **DISTRIBUTION:** PNG, throughout the Indo-Pacific. **IDEAL LENS:** 60–105 mm.

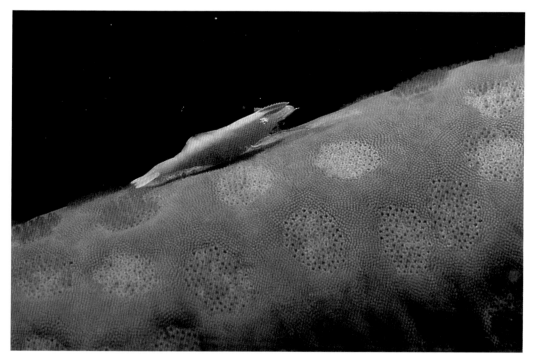

The Sea-star Shrimp (*Periclimenes soror*) utilises a variety of sea stars, including the Blue Sea Star, as hosts. To avoid detection, it generally adopts the colouration of the host species.
DEPTH RANGE: 1–20 m (3–65 ft). **DISTRIBUTION:** PNG, throughout the Indo-Pacific. **IDEAL LENS:** 105 mm.

A fairly common sea star, *Nardoa novaecaledoniae* is found in the shallows on living reefs. It often hosts the parasitic sea snail *Thyca stellasteris* and the Sea-star Shrimp (*Periclimenes soror*), both shown opposite.
DEPTH RANGE: 2–5 m (6–15 ft). **DISTRIBUTION:** PNG, Australia, Solomon Islands, Indonesia, Philippines. **IDEAL LENS:** 24 mm.

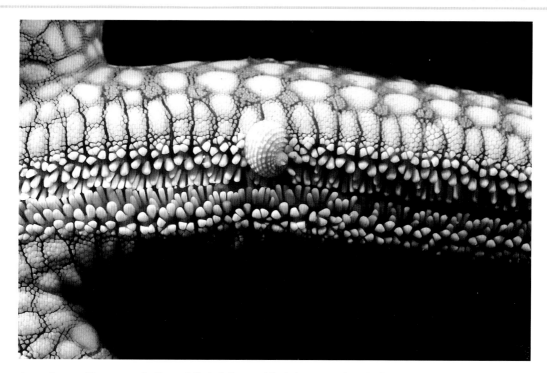

A small parasitic sea snail, *Thyca stellasteris* lives and feeds in among the tube feet on the underside of various sea stars, including *Nardoa novaecaledoniae*.

DEPTH RANGE: 1–20 m (3–65 ft). **DISTRIBUTION:** PNG, throughout the Indo-Pacific. **IDEAL LENS:** 105 mm.

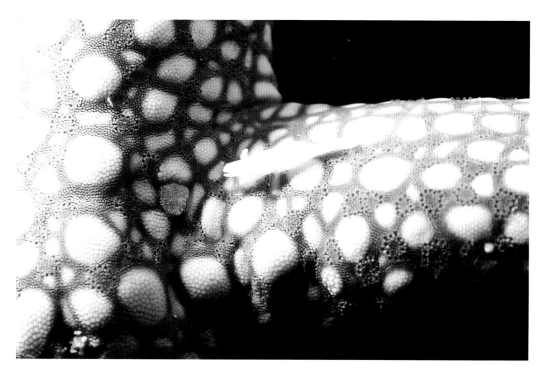

While many species in the *Periclimenes* genus have evolved close relationships with anemones and corals, the adaptable Sea-star Shrimp prefers sea stars. When startled it retreats to the sea star's underside to hide.

DEPTH RANGE: 1–20 m (3–65 ft). **DISTRIBUTION:** PNG, throughout the Indo-Pacific. **IDEAL LENS:** 105 mm.

The Bubble Coral (*Plerogyra sinuosa*) is an unusual hard coral generally found growing on the sides of rocks, on bommies or drop-offs. The grape-like vesicles can inflict a very nasty sting on humans and other creatures. **DEPTH RANGE:** 5–30 m (15–100 ft). **DISTRIBUTION:** PNG, throughout the Indo-Pacific. **IDEAL LENS:** 15–60 mm.

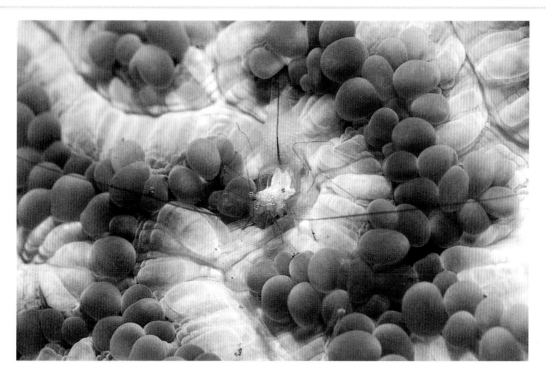

The exquisitely delicate Philippine Shrimp (*Vir philippinensis*) is able to find rich pickings among the folds and vesicles of the Bubble Corals that grow in Milne Bay, Papua New Guinea.
DEPTH RANGE: 5–30 m (15–100 ft). **DISTRIBUTION:** PNG, throughout the Indo-Pacific. **IDEAL LENS:** 105 mm.

The little shrimp featured here, and on the opposite page, is a species of *Periclimenes*. Less than 30 mm (1 in) long, it is characterised by an almost translucent body and fluorescent purple bands on its legs.
DEPTH RANGE: 5–30 m (15–100 ft). **DISTRIBUTION:** PNG, throughout the Indo-Pacific. **IDEAL LENS:** 105 mm.

Porites corals are found in the shallow waters of quiet bays or lagoons. Once they reach low-water levels the centre dies but slowly they grow outwards, their pitted surfaces anchoring a host of little creatures.
DEPTH RANGE: 2–20 m (6–65 ft). **DISTRIBUTION:** PNG, much of the Indo-Pacific. **IDEAL LENS:** 15–24 mm.

The larvae of the tiny but spectacular Christmas-tree Worm (*Spirobranchus giganteus*) settle into minute crevices where coral polyps have died. The worms secrete a tube of calcium carbonate, into which they retreat at low tide, but once covered with water, they stretch out their filamentous arms like a minature pine tree. (The Christmas-tree Worm is also pictured on pages 119 and 169.)
DEPTH RANGE: 2–10 m (6–35 ft).
DISTRIBUTION: PNG, much of the Indo-Pacific.
IDEAL LENS: 60–105 mm.

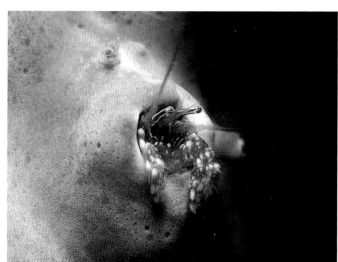

Harm's Coral Hermit Crab (*Paguritta harmsi*) is usually very quick to move into the old homes of departed Christmas-tree Worms. The crab's large feathery antennae filler out plankton from the passing water column.
DEPTH RANGE: 1–10 m (3–35 ft).
DISTRIBUTION: PNG, Solomon Islands, Australia.
IDEAL LENS: 105 mm with +2 dioptre.

Here a colony of *Serpulorbis grandis* worm snails has made its homesite on a mound of *Porites* coral. Worm snails cement their irregularly coiled shells to hard structures and 'fish' for plankton in a most industrious fashion. A close-up of the same species of worm snail can be seen on page 35.
DEPTH RANGE: 3–25 m (9–80 ft).
DISTRIBUTION: PNG, Australia, Philippines.
IDEAL LENS: 15–24 mm.

Corallimorpharians are more commonly known as jewel anemones because of their resemblance to anemones. They are, however, more closely related to hard corals, although they do not secrete calcium carbonate structures. Corallimorpharians inhabit shallow reefs and rubble patches. The Ballooning Corallimorpharian (*Amplexidiscus fenestrafer*) shown here is found singly or in colonies. Individuals can be up to 30 cm (12 in) in diameter. **DEPTH RANGE:** 3–15 m (9–45 ft). **DISTRIBUTION:** PNG, much of the Indo-Pacific. **IDEAL LENS:** 20–60 mm.

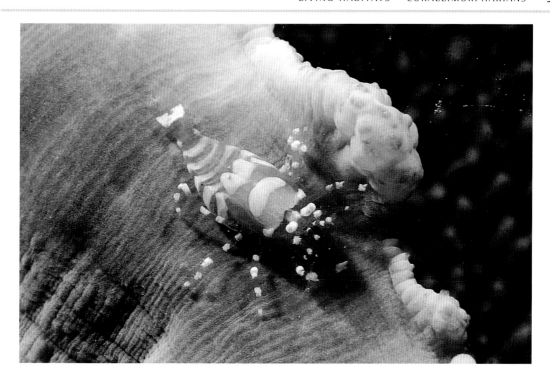

TOP AND ABOVE: The Furtive Shrimp (*Pliopontonia furtiva*) scavenges around the rim (top) and among the tentacles (above) of various corallimorpharians, including the Ballooning Corallimorpharian. Close examination of these living structures often reveals an array of other beautiful and interesting little creatures.

DEPTH RANGE: 3–15 m (9–45 ft). **DISTRIBUTION:** PNG, throughout the Indo-Pacific. **IDEAL LENS:** 105 mm.

The common basket star *Astroboa nuda* is nocturnal. By day it hides beneath a rock or among living colonies but come night it stretches its multi-branched arms out into the water column in order to catch plankton. A variety of other animals avail themselves of the basket star's reach to capture their own food.

DEPTH RANGE: 1–10 m (3–35 ft). **DISTRIBUTION:** PNG, much of the Indo-Pacific region. **IDEAL LENS:** 15–24 mm.

Basket stars often creep up to the top of *Porites* coral to 'fish' at night. Here, another *Porites* inhabitant and 'fisher', the worm snail *Serpulorbis grandis* (see also on page 31), employs a different strategy for capturing food in the passing current. It spits out a web of mucus, often catching the finer particles missed by the arms of neighbouring basket stars.
DEPTH RANGE: 3–25 m (9–80 ft). **DISTRIBUTION:** PNG, Australia, Philippines. **IDEAL LENS:** 60 mm.

The Basket-star Shrimp (*Periclimenses lanipes*) is often found in association with the large basket stars *Astroboa nuda* and *A. granulatus*. Like their nocturnal hosts, these shrimps are very shy of the torchlight and are hard to photograph.
DEPTH RANGE: 1–10 m (3–35 ft). **DISTRIBUTION:** PNG. **IDEAL LENS:** 105 mm.

Sea whips, like sea fans, are gorgonians; only in their single-stemmed shape do they essentially differ. Found on rocky coral reefs and drop-offs, the Red Sea Whip (*Ellisella* sp.) plays host to many small creatures. Especially well accommodated are those with a longitudinal axis — for obvious reasons.

DEPTH RANGE: 5–30 m (15–100 ft). **DISTRIBUTION:** PNG, throughout the Indo-Pacific. **IDEAL LENS:** 13–20 mm.

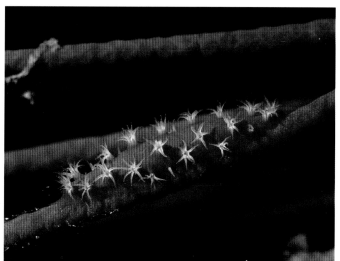

The small allied cowry *Aclyvolva lanceolata* lives and feeds on the Red Sea Whip. This cowry has a most unusual mantle with 'polyps' which mimic the appearance of its host when its polyps are extended. In the next photo both cowry and host have retracted their polyps.
DEPTH RANGE: 5–30 m (15–100 ft).
DISTRIBUTION: PNG, throughout the Indo-Pacific.
IDEAL LENS: 105 mm.

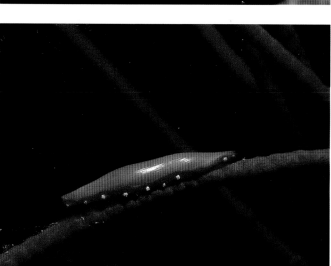

Still more remarkable, these 'polyps' are able to retract themselves when the sea fan's polyps are not feeding.
DEPTH RANGE: 5–30 m (15–100 ft).
DISTRIBUTION: PNG, throughout the Indo-Pacific.
IDEAL LENS: 105 mm.

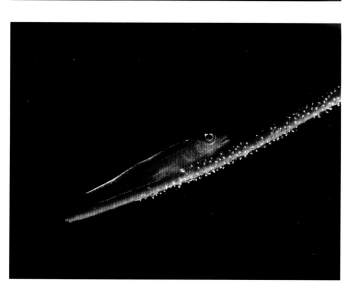

This goby, a species of *Bryaninops*, is equipped with cup-like pelvic fins which can be used to create suction between the fish and the Red Sea Whip. In this way the goby can remain lodged even in the strongest current.
DEPTH RANGE: 5–30 m (15–100 ft).
DISTRIBUTION: PNG, throughout the Indo-Pacific.
IDEAL LENS: 105 mm.

Sea fans (sometimes known as gorgonians) look like plants but they are actually colonies of polyps that live on a branched structure near strong currents. When the tentacles of the polyps are extended, as with this species of *Muricella*, they are often brightly coloured.

DEPTH RANGE: 13–40 m+ (39–120 ft+).
DISTRIBUTION: PNG, Indonesia, Australia.
IDEAL LENS: 15 mm.

With its polyps retracted, the same sea fan looks grey and bland. The whole colony has now shut down its feeding activity. Under no circumstances should you touch sea fans as this will cause parts to die off and eventually the whole colony will die.

DEPTH RANGE: 13–40 m+ (39–120 ft+).
DISTRIBUTION: PNG, Indonesia, Australia.
IDEAL LENS: 15 mm.

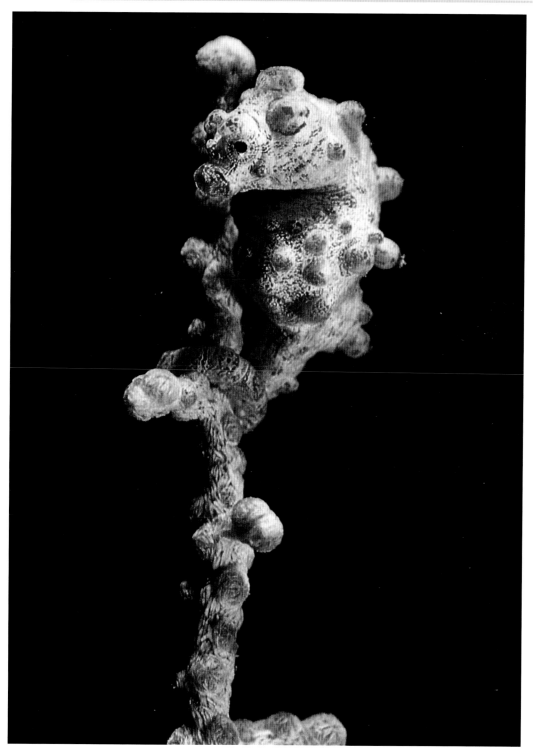

The Pygmy Seahorse (*Hippocampus bargabanti*) blends into its host sea fan almost perfectly. It is one of only a few seahorses that enjoy strong currents. By tightly gripping the ends of the fan's 'branch' with its tail it is able to reach out into the water to feed. It may take a lengthy dive to locate this seahorse and it is extremely difficult to find; it only inhabits *Muricella* species and can be recognised by its pink spots. (See page 172 for another view of this seahorse.)
DEPTH RANGE: 15–40 m+ (45–125 ft+). **DISTRIBUTION:** PNG, Indonesia, Australia. **IDEAL LENS:** 105 mm with +2 dioptre.

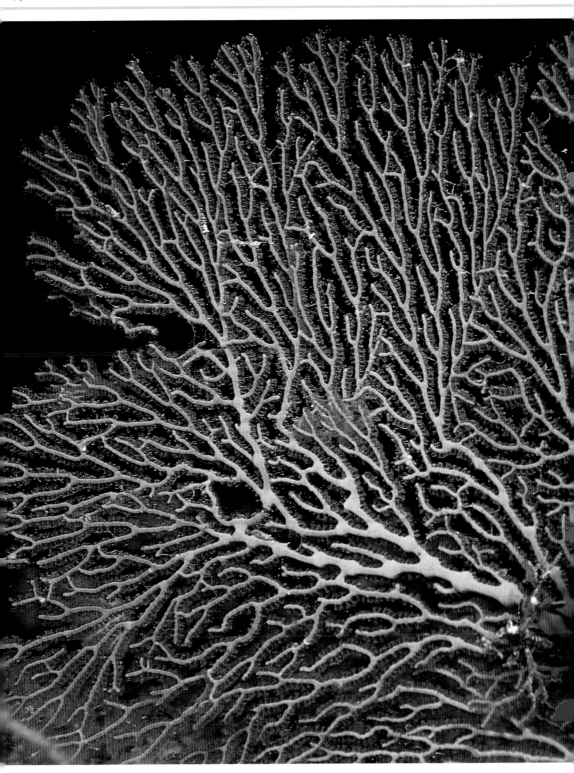

The Orange Sea Fan, a species of *Melithaea*, is another sea fan worth investigation when diving among coral reefs. It is relatively common on drop-offs or steep sloping reefs and reef-tops, providing homes and/or food for a number of small creatures.

DEPTH RANGE: 5–40 m+ (15–120 ft+). **DISTRIBUTION:** PNG, throughout the western Indo-Pacific. **IDEAL LENS:** 15–24 mm.

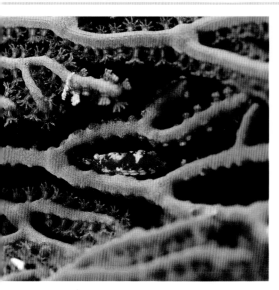

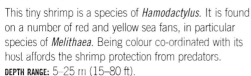

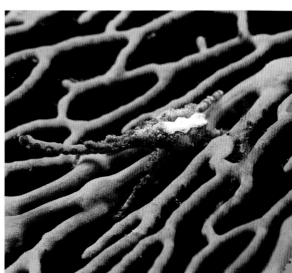

This tiny shrimp is a species of *Hamodactylus*. It is found on a number of red and yellow sea fans, in particular species of *Melithaea*. Being colour co-ordinated with its host affords the shrimp protection from predators.
DEPTH RANGE: 5–25 m (15–80 ft).
DISTRIBUTION: PNG, throughout the Indo-Pacific.
IDEAL LENS: 105 mm with +2 or +4 dioptre.

The Gorgonian Crab (*Xenocarcinus depressus*), shown here on *Melithaea* branches, is also featured on page 23.
DEPTH RANGE: 5–25 m (15–80 ft).
DISTRIBUTION: PNG, tropical Indian Ocean–western Pacific including Indonesia, Philippines, Australia, Fiji, Solomon Islands.
IDEAL LENS: 60–105 mm.

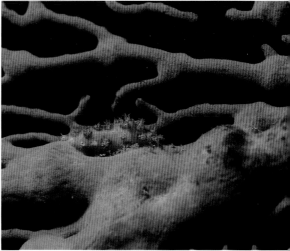

Unperturbed by the strong current, this cowry of the genus *Primovula* browses methodically along the branches of a yellow sea fan, a species of *Melithaea*.
DEPTH RANGE: 9 m (30 ft).
DISTRIBUTION: PNG.
IDEAL LENS: 105 mm.

The spindle cowry *Prosimnia semperi* feeds on a species of *Melithaea*. Spindle cowries are frequently found among sea fans but they are not easy to spot.
DEPTH RANGE: 5–30 m (15–100 ft).
DISTRIBUTION: PNG, Australia, Fiji, Philippines, Japan.
IDEAL LENS: 105 mm.

Here the polyps of Red Gorgonian (*Acabaria* sp.) have spread their tentacles wide. Growing on rock walls and reef-tops, this sea fan is the favourite host of the small Red Allied Cowry (*Crenavolva striatula*).
DEPTH RANGE: 1–6 m (3–20 ft). **DISTRIBUTION:** PNG. **IDEAL LENS:** 15 mm.

The spectacular Red Allied Cowry is beautifully matched to the Red Gorgonian on which it lives and feeds. Its bumpy shell, too, mimics the knobbly branches of this sea fan.
DEPTH RANGE: 3–40 m (9–125 ft). **DISTRIBUTION:** PNG, throughout the Indo-Pacific. **IDEAL LENS:** 105 mm.

This labyrinth-like sea fan spreads its branches wide but remains securely anchored to its hard surface. Found on drop-offs and reef-tops this unidentified species plays host to the small allied cowry shown below.
DEPTH RANGE: 3–30 m (9–100 ft). **DISTRIBUTION:** PNG, much of the central Indo-Pacific. **IDEAL LENS:** 15 mm.

You will need to look hard at this photograph, and still harder at the real thing, to make out the form of an allied cowry along this section of the above sea fan.
DEPTH RANGE: 5–20 m (15–65 ft). **DISTRIBUTION:** PNG, Solomon Islands, Australia. **IDEAL LENS:** 60 mm.

Subergorgia mollis is a massive pink sea fan that favours reef slopes and steep drop-offs, making it an ideal subject for wide-angle photography. This specimen is about 2.5 m (8 ft) across.
DEPTH RANGE: 3–30 m (9–100 ft). **DISTRIBUTION:** PNG, much of the central Indo-Pacific. **IDEAL LENS:** 15 mm.

A slender spindle cowry of the genus *Hiata* laboriously makes its way along a main branch of the *Subgorgia mollis* sea fan. Its almost perfect match ensures its safety.
DEPTH RANGE: 3–30 m (9–100 ft). **DISTRIBUTION:** PNG, much of the central Indo-Pacific. **IDEAL LENS:** 60 mm.

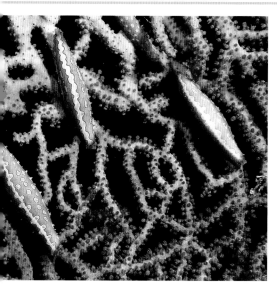

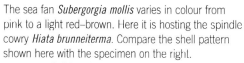

The sea fan *Subergorgia mollis* varies in colour from pink to a light red–brown. Here it is hosting the spindle cowry *Hiata brunneiterma*. Compare the shell pattern shown here with the specimen on the right.
DEPTH RANGE: 3–30 m (9–100 ft).
DISTRIBUTION: PNG, most of the eastern Pacific.
IDEAL LENS: 15 mm.

Another specimen of the spindle cowry *Hiata brunneiterma*, also on the sea fan *Subergorgia mollis*, displays a reticulated pattern on its shell, deceptively different from the pattern on the left.
DEPTH RANGE: 3 30 m (9 100 ft).
DISTRIBUTION: PNG, most of the eastern Pacific.
IDEAL LENS: 60 mm.

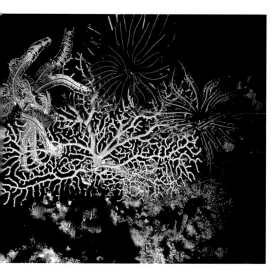

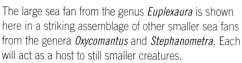

The large sea fan from the genus *Euplexaura* is shown here in a striking assemblage of other smaller sea fans from the genera *Oxycomantus* and *Stephanometra*. Each will act as a host to still smaller creatures.
DEPTH RANGE: 3–40 m+ (9–125 ft+).
DISTRIBUTION: PNG, Indonesia, Australia.
IDEAL LENS: 24 mm.

The Allied Tiger Cowry (*Crenavolva tigris*) frequents species of *Euplexaura*. Its striking pattern and colour make it an excellent photographic subject.
DEPTH RANGE: 5–40 m+ (15–125 ft+).
DISTRIBUTION: PNG, Japan, Indonesia, Thailand, Australia.
IDEAL LENS: 105 mm.

Colour on the reef is often a misleading identification characteristic. This unidentified sea fan appears green in natural light when growing on the top of live reefs but in deeper water, as here, it appears red.
DEPTH RANGE: 5–25 m (15–80 ft). **DISTRIBUTION:** PNG. **IDEAL LENS:** 15 mm.

This slender allied cowry (*Phenacovolva tokioi*) shot from above is relatively conspicuous but the same individual on the same sea fan when photographed from the side is easily missed.
DEPTH RANGE: 5–25 m (15–80 ft). **DISTRIBUTION:** PNG, much of the central Indo-Pacific. **IDEAL LENS:** 60 mm.

CHAPTER 2
COWRIES

Probably no other group of shelled creatures has the universal appeal of the cowries. Ranging from a few millimetres to over 100 mm (4 in) in length, they are prized by collectors for the striking colours and patterns of their enamelled shell, but the animals have more to offer than just an attractive shell. They have a graceful form and are often brightly coloured, with long eye-bearing tentacles and a mantle divided into two fleshy lobes that meet across the back of the shell. Cowries are difficult to identify to species level until the mantle is retracted and the shell revealed. Ranging from mudflats to open coral reefs, some of these molluscs live on other creatures. They hide on the underside of rocks and corals by day and by night feed on algae, sponges and hydroids. Curiously, some species are in evidence year-round, while others seem to disappear at certain times.

The Tiger Cowry (*Cypraea tigris*) is found in almost all habitats in shallow tropical waters.
DEPTH RANGE: 2–10 m (6–35 ft). **DISTRIBUTION:** PNG, much of the Indo-Pacific. **IDEAL LENS:** 60 mm.

White-shelled and strongly pear-shaped, the Ivory Cowry (*Cypraea eburnea*) has an elaborate grey and white mantle. It is often found in soft sand or silt bottoms, frequently in small clusters on logs or debris.
DEPTH RANGE: 5–30 m (15–100 ft).
DISTRIBUTION: PNG, Australia, Indonesia.
IDEAL LENS: 60 mm.

The Zigzag Cowry (*Cypraea ziczac*) appears to forage by both day and night. Its bright red mantle is even more spectacular than its shell, which is orange and boldly ornamented with zigzag yellow lines, although some colour variation is found throughout its range.
DEPTH RANGE: 2–20 m (6–65 ft).
DISTRIBUTION: PNG, much of the Indo-Pacific.
IDEAL LENS: 60–105 mm.

With an eye-catching pink–red mantle, *Cypraea chinensis* is an attractive cowry. Its shell has a beige base, pale violet spots on the sides and over the margins, and the top is light brown with orange speckles.
DEPTH RANGE: 5–20 m (15–65 ft).
DISTRIBUTION: PNG, the central Indo-Pacific.
IDEAL LENS: 60 mm.

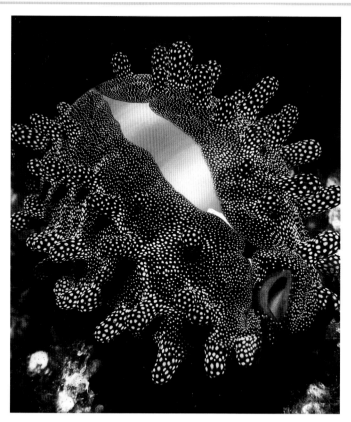

With its magnificent green-speckled mantle almost covering the shell, the Mole Cowry (*Cypraea talpa*) is pictured here in its nightwear. During the day its mantle is retracted, revealing a highly polished shell with a dark chocolate brown base and sides, and a pale brown top with three light creamy brown bands. This cowry may be found in seaweed on reefs and rubble bottoms.

DEPTH RANGE: 3–25 m (9–85 ft).
DISTRIBUTION: PNG, throughout the Indo-Pacific.
IDEAL LENS: 60 mm.

Easily identified by the prominent white spots on its shell, the Tan and White Cowry (*Cypraea cribraria*) has a reddish brown pear-shaped shell with a white margin. Its mantle is a pretty cerise to vermillion red. This cowry is often found in association with red encrusting sponges.

DEPTH RANGE: 3–20 m (9–65 ft).
DISTRIBUTION: PNG, throughout the Indo-Pacific.
IDEAL LENS: 60 mm.

CHAPTER 3

SEA SLUGS

Although relatives of the garden snail, sea slugs are characterised by having an internal or reduced shell or no shell at all. All are hermaphrodites and produce prodigious quantities of eggs, which they deposit on algae or sponges. Behind the eyes they bear a pair of tubular tentacles called rhinophores. The 'foot' may be lobed and some sea slugs bear fleshy projections from the mantle called cerata, which contain exensions of the gut and are used in defence. In this group, it is the gorgeous colours and graceful forms of nudibranchs that so impress underwater photographers. Their flavours, however, are less nice; many secrete foul substances when attacked, others deter predators with the stinging cells of hydroids upon which they have fed. Nudibranchs live in almost all reef habitats. Most are 3–10 cm (1–4 in) long but some reach up to 50 cm (20 in) long. They eat sponges, hydroids, soft corals, gorgonians, ascidians and algae, and some take small crustaceans or fish.

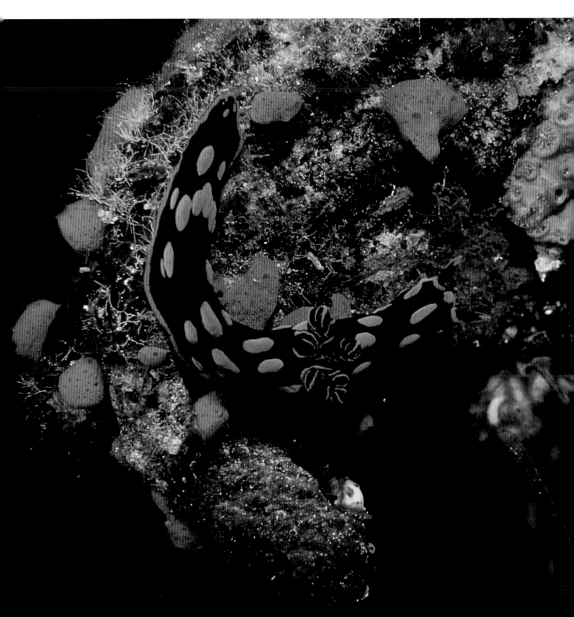

OPPOSITE AND ABOVE: Often reaching more than 120 mm (4.7 in) in length — a bit longer than a Mars Bar™ — the Dusky Nembrotha (*Nembrotha kubaryana*) is a large nudibranch. Looking like it is dressed up to go to a party, its appendages vary in colour from area to area. Sometimes its horn-like tentacles — its rhinophores — are red and its gills green, sometimes vice versa. This species feeds on ascidians and lives in colonies that inhabit steep reef slopes and drop-offs of the reef.

DEPTH RANGE: 5–30 m (15–100 ft). **DISTRIBUTION:** PNG. **IDEAL LENS:** 60–105 mm.

Looking here like a pile of decaying weed, the sea hare *Bursatella leachii* varies in shape and ornamentation from area to area. It is found on sandy silt slopes and flats, feeding mainly on thick mats and films of blue–green algae.
DEPTH RANGE: 5–25 m (15–80 ft). **DISTRIBUTION:** PNG, throughout the Indo-Pacific. **IDEAL LENS:** 60–105 mm.

Side-gilled slugs are close relatives of nudibranchs but have only one set of gills on their right side. This one, *Berthella martensi*, is often found on sandy rocky bottoms feeding on sponges. It varies widely in colour and has the remarkable ability to break off large sections of its mantle in order to escape a predator.
DEPTH RANGE: 3–20 m (9–65 ft). **DISTRIBUTION:** PNG, throughout the Indo-Pacific. **IDEAL LENS:** 60 mm.

The delicate fan-like extensions of this Sap-sucking Slug (*Cyerce nigricans*) are in fact part of its gut. They wave about as the creature moves along, providing a large surface area for its respiration. This slug slices open algae and sucks up the contents of individual cells. It produces distasteful secretions and discards part of its external gut if harassed. Its eggs are laid in masses of flattened spirals.
DEPTH RANGE: 3–30 m (9–100 ft).
DISTRIBUTION: PNG, Africa–Australia, Indonesia.
IDEAL LENS: 60–105 mm.

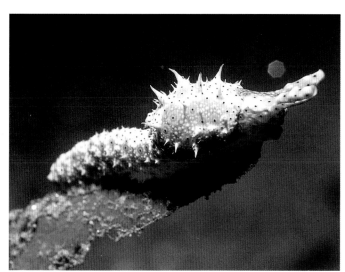

Dotted and spotted and covered in horny bumps, the cell-sucking slug *Lobiger souverbii* is found in the shallows, feeding on green weeds.
DEPTH RANGE: 1–6 m (3–20 ft).
DISTRIBUTION: PNG, Indonesia, Solomon Islands.
IDEAL LENS: 105 mm.

Almost transparent, the cell-sucking slug *Elysia ornata* is often found in association with green algae from the genus *Bryopsis* on shallow reef areas and rubble bottoms. Typically covered with numerous black and white dots, its mantle is edged in black with inner orange and yellow bands that may be separated by a white line. This banding is often repeated on the tips of the rhinophores.
DEPTH RANGE: 2–10 m (6–35 ft).
DISTRIBUTION: PNG.
IDEAL LENS: 60–105 mm.

The candy-striped Bordered Tambja (*Tambja affinis*) lives around open reefs and drop-offs. Like the cunjevoi shown here, it forages in places where strong currents sweep in food particles.
DEPTH RANGE: 5–25 m (15–80 ft). **DISTRIBUTION:** PNG, throughout the Indo-Pacific. **IDEAL LENS:** 60–105 mm.

Although this nudibranch from the genus *Notodoris* is relatively common, it remains undescribed. It can be found on reef edges and drop-offs, feeding on calcareous sponges from the genus *Leucetta*.
DEPTH RANGE: 5–20 m (15–65 ft). **DISTRIBUTION:** PNG, throughout the Indo-Pacific. **IDEAL LENS:** 60–105 mm.

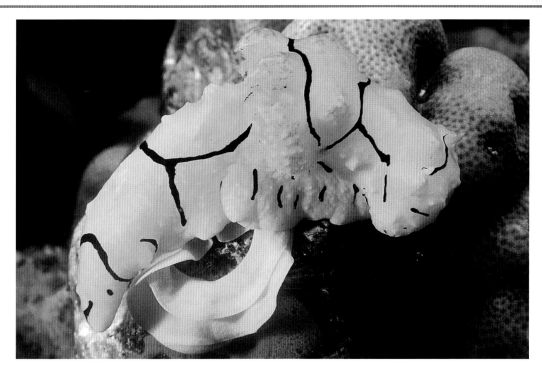

Caught by the camera in a remarkable moment, the nudibranch *Notodoris minor* is laying its eggs in a long, flat continuous ribbon. Bright yellow with fine black lines, this nudibranch is found on reefs and drop-offs where it feeds on calcareous sponges, somehow separating the sponge's spicules from its edible tissue.
DEPTH RANGE: 5–20 m (15–65 ft). **DISTRIBUTION:** PNG, throughout the Indo-Pacific. **IDEAL LENS:** 60–105 mm.

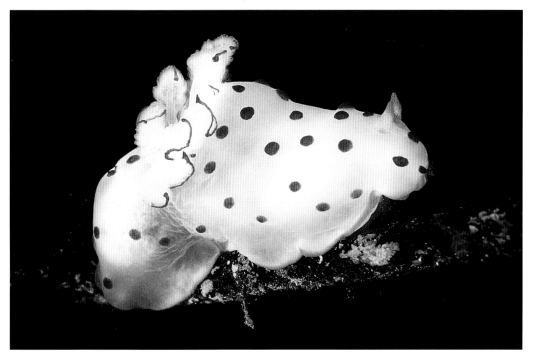

Gymnodoris ceylonica is so translucent that, with the right lighting, its internal organs become visible. Its 20–40 eggs are laid in loosely-spiralled masses upon seaweed or rubble bottoms. (This nudibranch also appears on page 166.)
DEPTH RANGE: 3–30 m (9–100 ft). **DISTRIBUTION:** PNG, Africa–Australia–Japan. **IDEAL LENS:** 60 mm.

The beautiful Spanish Dancer (*Hexabranchus sanguineus*) is much larger than most nudibranchs — sometimes over 45 cm (18 in) long. It varies in colour from light pink to flame red and is most often found at night on reef-tops, slopes and drop-offs, although smaller specimens sometimes appear during the day.

DEPTH RANGE: 1–40 m+ (3–125 ft+). **DISTRIBUTION:** PNG and much of the Indo-Pacific. **IDEAL LENS:** 15–60 mm.

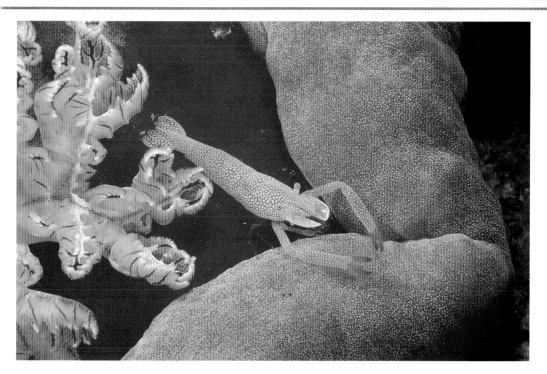

This Spanish Dancer is hosting an Imperial Shrimp (*Periclimenes imperator*). The Imperial Shrimp is an opportunist of the first order, happy to exploit the living habitats of many different hosts.

DEPTH RANGE: 1–25 m+ (3–80 ft+). **DISTRIBUTION:** PNG and most of the Indo-Pacific. **IDEAL LENS:** 105 mm.

This juvenile Yellow Margined Snapper (*Lutjanus fulvus*) has been caught unawares napping among the colourful eggs of the Spanish Dancer. Laid in their thousands in ribbon-like strips, these eggs are toxic to predators such as fish.

DEPTH RANGE: 6 m (20 ft). **DISTRIBUTION:** PNG. **IDEAL LENS:** 105 mm.

The nudibranch *Chromodoris elisabethina* is a member of the chromodorid family. Like the other members of its family, it feeds on sponges and is able to employ the sponges' poisonous chemicals in its own defence. It grazes along the reef faces and drop-offs, as well as in the rubble areas.

DEPTH RANGE: 3–30 m (9–100 ft). **DISTRIBUTION:** PNG, throughout the Indo-Pacific. **IDEAL LENS:** 60–105 mm.

Another member of the genus *Chromodoris* shares this family's defence strategies but it inhabits only the rubble bottoms. Note its similarity to *C. tinctoria* on page 60.

DEPTH RANGE: 5 m (15 ft). **DISTRIBUTION:** PNG. **IDEAL LENS:** 60 mm.

A creature of open reefs, drop-offs and rubble areas, Kunie's Chromodoris (*Chromodoris kuniei*) is another striking nudibranch species. Although similarly coloured to *C. leopardus*, *C. geminus* and *Risbecia tryoni*, the mantle of Kunie's Chromodoris is characterised by a broad band comprising three slightly different shades of purple along its edge.
DEPTH RANGE: 3–30 m (9–100 ft). **DISTRIBUTION:** PNG, throughout the Indo-Pacific. **IDEAL LENS:** 60–100 mm.

Although closely resembling *Chromodoris geometrica* and once thought to be a colour variation, the recently named *C. hintuanensis* differs in gill and rhinopore colour and has small white rounded mantle nodules edged with magenta.
DEPTH RANGE: 6 m (20 ft). **DISTRIBUTION:** PNG. **IDEAL LENS:** 105 mm.

This nudibranch, *Chromodoris tinctoria*, is usually found foraging around sandy rubble areas. It is always speckled red, and has a yellow mantle edge, but the white submarginal band shown here is not always present.
DEPTH RANGE: 3–10 m (9–35 ft). **DISTRIBUTION:** PNG, throughout the Indo-Pacific. **IDEAL LENS:** 60–105 mm.

Looking here like a fried egg with rhinophores, the red and orange spots of the nudibranch *Chromodoris daphne* are a warning to potential fish predators of its store of toxic chemicals. This is another occupant of sandy rubble areas.
DEPTH RANGE: 1–10 m (3–35 ft). **DISTRIBUTION:** PNG, Australia, Indonesia. **IDEAL LENS:** 60 mm.

Chromodoris leopardus is distinguished from the similar-coloured *C. kuniei*, *C. germinus* and *Risbecia tryoni* by its leopard-like spots. It moves along rubble bottoms by 'flapping' the anterior end of its mantle.
DEPTH RANGE: 2–30 m (6–100 ft). **DISTRIBUTION:** PNG, Australia, Philippines. **IDEAL LENS:** 60 mm.

Harder to spot than most nudibranchs because of its clever colouring, this species of *Gymnodoris* grazes upon algae that grow upon the coralline alga *Halimeda macroloba*.
DEPTH RANGE: 10 m (35 ft).
DISTRIBUTION: PNG.
IDEAL LENS: 60 mm.

The spotted nudibranch *Risbecia tryoni* is often found in pairs 'tailgating' along the bottom. One nudibranch finds the other by following its mucous trail and they remain a pair as long as the follower keeps in contact with the leader's tail. Often the Imperial Shrimp (*Periclimenes imperator*) hitches a ride, not only feasting on the goodies exposed when the sea floor is disturbed by the moving nudibranch, but also gaining protection from predators.

DEPTH RANGE: 2–10 m (6–35 ft). **DISTRIBUTION:** PNG, Malaysia, Australia through to Tasmania. **IDEAL LENS:** 60 mm.

With diagonal black lines, purple- and yellow-tinged blotches and red–orange gills and rhinophores, *Hypselodoris nigrostriata* is a striking nudibranch. The similar-looking *H. zephyra* differs by having parallel black lines on the mantle and gills that are a uniform orange.

DEPTH RANGE: 3–20 m (9–65 ft).
DISTRIBUTION: PNG, Thailand, Indonesia.
IDEAL LENS: 60 mm.

This warty, spotted species of the *Kentrodoris* genus is a nudibranch that is often found in pairs on rubble bottoms.

DEPTH RANGE: 2–15 m (6–50 ft).
DISTRIBUTION: PNG, Philippines.
IDEAL LENS: 105 mm.

While always colourfully clad, the nudibranch *Hypselodoris infucata* displays considerable regional variation in appearance. Juveniles often lack the dark specks and have relatively large yellow patches. Once again, this is an inhabitant of sand and rubble areas.

DEPTH RANGE: 2–30 m (6–100 ft).
DISTRIBUTION: PNG, throughout the Indo-Pacific.
IDEAL LENS: 60–105 mm.

This nudibranch, *Hypselodoris bullockii*, displays a variation of colours, depending on where it is found. The colour of its mantle ranges from pale yellow or white to a deep purple, with a fine opaque white line along the edge or a reddish purple border. The gills and rhinophores are yellow–orange with a pink or purple band at the base.
DEPTH RANGE: 3–30 m (9–100 ft). **DISTRIBUTION:** PNG, Indonesia, Thailand, Australia, Malaysia. **IDEAL LENS:** 60 mm.

Seen here crawling over *Halimeda cylindrica* is the nudibranch *Hypselodoris mouaci*. This is a creature of shallow rubble bottoms where delectable algae proliferate and upon which it grazes.
DEPTH RANGE: 1–10 m (3–35 ft). **DISTRIBUTION:** PNG, Africa–Australia–Hawaii. **IDEAL LENS:** 105 mm.

Looking like a marzipan ornament for a Christmas cake, this nudibranch of the genus *Noumea* is quite distinctive. It was found feeding in the shallows on a sandy silt bottom but it is rarely seen in the area where this photograph was taken and little is known of its habits.

DEPTH RANGE: 2 m (6 ft).
DISTRIBUTION: PNG.
IDEAL LENS: 105 mm.

A follower of the adage that 'blue and green should never be seen except with yellow in-between', the nudibranch *Ceratosoma sinuata* also comes in many other colours and patterns. It lays white to pale blue or purple egg ribbons and feeds among shallow reefs and along rubble bottoms.

DEPTH RANGE: 3–15 m (9–50 ft).
DISTRIBUTION: PNG, throughout the Indo-Pacific.
IDEAL LENS: 60–105 mm.

Though a sponge-grazer, *Discodoris boholiensis* is often seen crawling about in the open, preferring sandy rubble habitats. It is distinguished by the narrow longitudinal crest between the rhinophores and gills, the small tubercles on the mantle and a wide skirt which may be broken off when disturbed. It is often observed in company with the Imperial Shrimp (*Periclimenes imperator*).

DEPTH RANGE: 1–15 m (3–50 ft).
DISTRIBUTION: PNG, throughout the Indo-Pacific.
IDEAL LENS: 60–105 mm.

The tubercles studding the mantle of this nudibranch species of *Mexichromis* look as if their tips have been dipped in brilliant Indian ink. Its mantle is fringed with either orange or purple spots. The tubercles of the similar-looking *M. multituberculata* are more scattered and those of *M. mariei* and *M. festiva* are reduced to rounded papillae. *M. macropus* also has pointed tubercles but its mantle is edged with radial orange–yellow stripes.

DEPTH RANGE: 10–40 m (35–125 ft).
DISTRIBUTION: PNG, Australia, Indonesia.
IDEAL LENS: 60 mm.

Like other species of *Ceratosoma*, *C. tenue* has a long curved dorsal 'horn' which acts as a lure, attracting potential predators to the part of its body that is packed with nasty-tasting chemicals. Distinguishing it from the similar-looking *C. trilobatum*, *C. tenue* has three mantle lobes on each side of its body. This nudibranch has a hard body (where most are soft) and comes in a wide variety of colours. It is usually found in sandy rubble areas.

DEPTH RANGE: 2–10 m (6–35 ft).
DISTRIBUTION: PNG, throughout the Indo-Pacific.
IDEAL LENS: 60 mm.

White with bright glowing orange trim around its generous skirt, the nudibranch *Glossodoris averni* cruises around the sandy rubble zones and weedy areas in search of food.

DEPTH RANGE: 3–15 m (9–80 ft).
DISTRIBUTION: PNG, Africa, Indonesia, northern Australia.
IDEAL LENS: 60 mm.

The nudibranch *Glossodoris cincta* discharges a milky fluid from its gill area when disturbed. Its colouring depends on where it is found. For example, those from the Red Sea have quite dark colouring while those from the Maldives to northern Australia are lighter around the skirt.
DEPTH RANGE: 3–15 m (9–50 ft). **DISTRIBUTION:** PNG, Australia, Fiji, Indonesia–Africa. **IDEAL LENS:** 60 mm.

Pictured here is a rare yellow form of *Glossodoris atromarginata*, which is usually white with a black or brown edge. The frilliness of the mantle edge varies between individuals. This is an inhabitant of both coral reefs and rubble areas.
DEPTH RANGE: 3–20 m (9–65 ft). **DISTRIBUTION:** PNG, throughout the Indo-Pacific. **IDEAL LENS:** 60–105 mm.

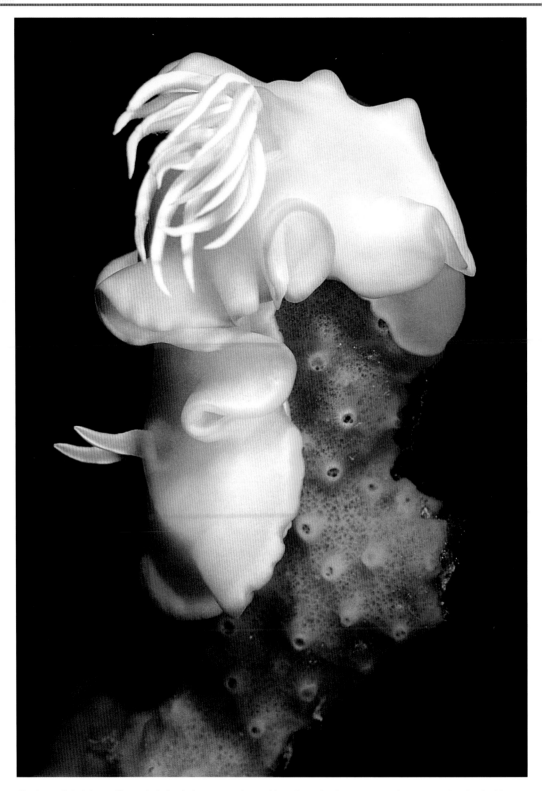

The beautiful white nudibranch *Ardeadoris egretta*, pictured here investigating a sponge, has a mantle edged with yellow. It can be found on open reef-tops and gentle slopes.
DEPTH RANGE: 5–15 m (15–50 ft). **DISTRIBUTION:** PNG, Australia, Philippines–Japan. **IDEAL LENS:** 60–105 mm.

The beautifully-spotted white-and-black nudibranch Funeral Jorunna or Funeral Nudibranch (*Jorunna funebris*) is a popular photographic subject. Found in shallow waters on open reefs and rubble areas, it feeds on sponges.
DEPTH RANGE: 2–10 m (6–35 ft). DISTRIBUTION: PNG. IDEAL LENS: 60–105 mm.

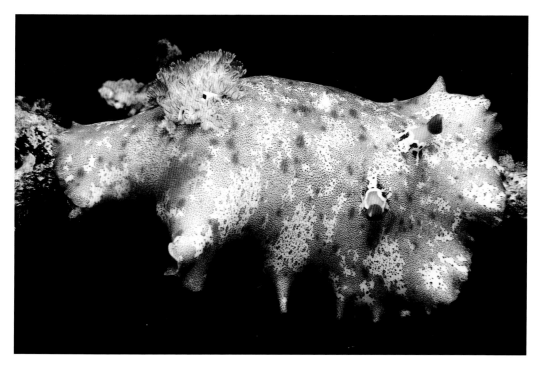

Rather more thick-set than most nudibranchs, *Platydoris formosa* has a hard, rigid mantle. It is found mostly at night and seems to like rubble to reef bottoms, where it displays great variation in colour.
DEPTH RANGE: 3–15 m (15–50 ft). DISTRIBUTION: PNG, much of the Pacific. IDEAL LENS: 60 mm.

Densely-coated in brown or yellowish brown pustules with a delicate, undulating mantle skirt, *Hoplodoris nodulosa* lives in shallow water. It characteristically has a smooth or almost smooth patch behind the rhinophores.
DEPTH RANGE: 1–6 m (3–20 ft). **DISTRIBUTION:** PNG, Australia, Japan, Indonesia. **IDEAL LENS:** 105 mm.

This very knobbly nudibranch, *Asteronotus cespitosus*, can be found in dead reef, rubble and sandy areas. Like so many of these nudibranchs, it varies in colour depending on its environment.
DEPTH RANGE: 2–20 m (6–65 ft). **DISTRIBUTION:** PNG, throughout the Indo-Pacific. **IDEAL LENS:** 60 mm.

The Ocellate Phyllidia (*Phyllidia ocellata*) is sometimes white with yellow tubercles and sometimes yellow with white tubercles, but always with a mantle decorated with black rings and patches. This nudibranch secretes digestive enzymes into sponges then sucks up the tenderised tissue.
DEPTH RANGE: 5–40 m (15–125 ft). **DISTRIBUTION:** PNG, throughout the Indo-Pacific. **IDEAL LENS:** 60–105 mm.

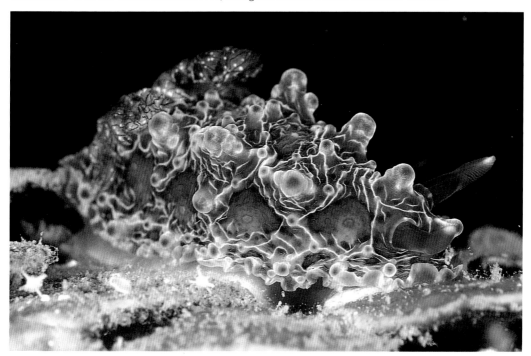

Though varying in colour from place to place, the almost translucent *Dendrodoris denisoni* always has its electric blue spots. A nudibranch of both cold and tropical waters, it feeds on rubble bottoms and sandy weed areas.
DEPTH RANGE: 3–20 m (9–65 ft). **DISTRIBUTION:** PNG, Australia, South Africa, New Zealand. **IDEAL LENS:** 60 mm.

Favorinus tsurganus was photographed feeding on the brownish ribbon-like eggs of another nudibranch species, which is apparently the main food source for this species. The rhinophores have three ring-like structures around them and the orange finger-like projections with black tips are actually its cerata, that is, externalities of the nudibranch's gut.

DEPTH RANGE: 1–10 m (3–35 ft).
DISTRIBUTION: PNG, Indonesia, Australia.
IDEAL LENS: 105 mm.

This delicately-striped sea slug is a species of *Armina*. It is usually found scouring sandy areas for its favourite food, soft corals and sea fans.

DEPTH RANGE: 8 m (25 ft).
DISTRIBUTION: PNG.
IDEAL LENS: 105 mm.

The mantle of this nudibranch, *Cuthona kanga,* is almost entirely adorned with 18–20 rows of cerata. Nudibranchs with cerata are devoid of gills as the cerata take over their function. This species is found in sandy weed areas where it feeds on a selection of hydroid species.

DEPTH RANGE: 3–30 m (9–100 ft).
DISTRIBUTION: PNG, Africa, Australia, Indonesia.
IDEAL LENS: 60–105 mm.

This swimming nudibranch with its full complement of cerata is a species of *Phidiana*. It cruises gracefully above soft sandy to silty bottoms in its endless search for hydroids.
DEPTH RANGE: 40 m (125 ft). **DISTRIBUTION:** PNG. **IDEAL LENS:** 60 mm.

This delicate and unusual nudibranch species of the genus *Flabellina* is found on rubble bottoms in very shallow water. It is seen here feeding on algae that cling to the *Halimeda* coralline algae.
DEPTH RANGE: 2 m (6 ft). **DISTRIBUTION:** PNG. **IDEAL LENS:** 105 mm.

The Blue Dragon (*Pteraeolidia ianthina*) has evolved ways of harnessing solar energy. While feeding on the solitary hydroid *Ralpharia* it swallows microscopic plants called zooxanthellae. Within the nudibranch the plants use the sun's energy to produce sugars, passing on a considerable portion to the nudibranch for its own use. Adults are blue to brownish purple. Juveniles are white. This species often gathers in clusters for 2–3 weeks around egg masses on large submerged rocks encrusted with coralline algae. This nudibranch can inflict a sting, using the hydroid's untriggered stinging cells in its body.

DEPTH RANGE: 1–30 m (3–100 ft). **DISTRIBUTION:** PNG, throughout the Indo-Pacific. **IDEAL LENS:** 60 mm.

Phyllodesmium longicirrum also gets much of its nutrition from its 'farm' of zooxanthellae, its many elongate cerata providing a large surface area for photosynthesis. Its cerata can be discarded to avoid capture.
(This nudibranch is also pictured on page 19.)
DEPTH RANGE: 5–25 m (15–80 ft). DISTRIBUTION: PNG, throughout the Indo-Pacific. IDEAL LENS: 20–60 mm.

The strange but beautiful Wondrous Melibe or Veil Nudibranch (*Melibe mirifica*) is capable of throwing its veil-like mouth out to entrap the small fish and crustaceans upon which it feeds, providing excellent video action.
DEPTH RANGE: 2–25 m (6–80 ft). DISTRIBUTION: PNG, the Indo-Pacific. IDEAL LENS: 24–60 mm.

CHAPTER 4

SCORPION-FISH

One popular underwater subject you will have no trouble recognising are the scorpion-fish. Within the scorpion-fish family are firefish, lionfish, waspfish, stingers and stonefish. All are equipped with venomous needle-sharp spines. In many species the venom is dangerous to humans, most notably in the Red Firefish and the Lionfish. The notorious Estuary and Reef Stonefish possess venom 10 times stronger than any other species. Scorpion-fish are generally sluggish, spending much of their time resting on the bottom. Many photographers have been inadvertently wounded by their spines, so beware. Always take care on sandy rubble bottoms and, when using a flash, be on the lookout for startled scorpion-fish which, in their attempt to flee, may inflict terrific pain. If you are wounded by a scorpion-fish, seek help quickly.

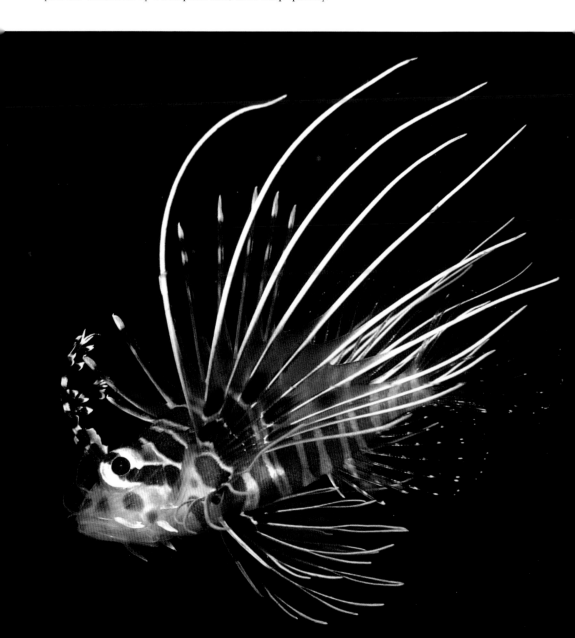

The pretty pink and apricot patterning of this Lacey Scorpion-fish (*Rhinopias aphanes*) is only one of the many colour variations in which it is found. Its filmy tentacles, skin flaps and changing colours provide such an effective camouflage that it can be hard to spot and is regarded as rare and something of a mystery.
DEPTH RANGE 5–40 m+ (15–125 ft+).
DISTRIBUTION: PNG, Australia, parts of the Indian Ocean.
IDEAL LENS: 60 mm.

Some scientists believe that the Lacey Scorpion-fish — also known as the Weedy or Merlet's Scorpion-fish — mimics crinoids on the reef. Note how the scorpion-fish lurks beside a large crinoid in the background of this picture.
DEPTH RANGE 5–40 m+ (15–125 ft+).
DISTRIBUTION: PNG, Australia, parts of the Indian Ocean.
IDEAL LENS: 60/105 mm.

OPPOSITE: Its white-rayed pectoral fins resembling angel-like wings, the Spotfin Lionfish (*Pterois antennata*), also known as Broadbarred Firefish, swims slowly but can devour a shrimp or crab in a split second. It hunts during the night, taking refuge in rocky crevices or coral during the day.
DEPTH RANGE: 3–30 m (9–100 ft). **DISTRIBUTION:** PNG, much of the Indo-Pacific. **IDEAL LENS:** 10–60 mm.

Seen here in one of its many striking colour variations is the Lacey Scorpion-fish (*Rhinopias aphanes*). Scorpion-fish will aggressively protect their young against predators. Hidden among this creature's decorative appendages are venomous dorsal spines.
DEPTH RANGE 5–40 m+ (15–125 ft+). **DISTRIBUTION:** PNG, Australia, parts of the Indian Ocean. **IDEAL LENS:** 60 mm.

Paisley-like patterns — this one in rich maroon — characterise the Lacey Scorpion-fish. Individuals tend to stay in the same spot for weeks or months, so local dive masters may learn their whereabouts.
DEPTH RANGE 5–40 m+ (15–125 ft+). **DISTRIBUTION:** PNG, Australia, parts of the Indian Ocean. **IDEAL LENS:** 60 mm.

Most species of *Rhinopias* slough off their outer layer of skin to help keep the body free of encrustations, parasites and algae. Note the loose, shedding skin on the pectoral fins of this Lacey Scorpion-fish.
DEPTH RANGE 5–40 m+ (15–125 ft+). **DISTRIBUTION:** PNG, Australia, parts of the Indian Ocean. **IDEAL LENS:** 60 mm.

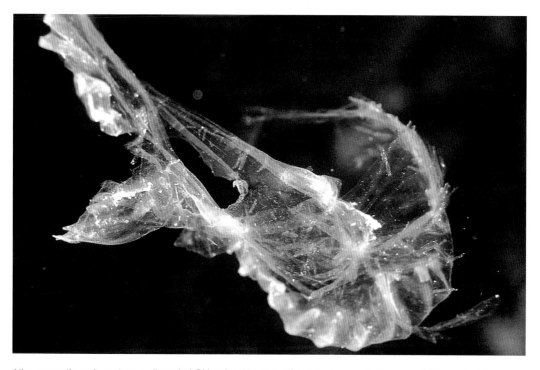

Like some ethereal creature, a discarded *Rhinopias* skin slips off and floats away in the current. These sheddings are quite frequent, with some individuals moulting as often as every 12 or 13 days.
DEPTH: RANGE: 5–40 m+ (15–125 ft+). **DISTRIBUTION:** PNG, Australia, parts of the Indian Ocean. **IDEAL LENS:** 60 mm.

The little-known Pink Weedy Scorpion-fish (*Rhinopias frondosa*), like other species of Rhinopias, crawls awkwardly along the bottom on its pelvic and pectoral fins and will sometimes 'hop' quickly towards its prey.
DEPTH RANGE: 5–40 m+ (15–125 ft+). **DISTRIBUTION:** PNG. **IDEAL LENS:** 60–24 mm.

A master of disguise, the Leaf Scorpion-fish (*Taenianotus triacanthus*) sits propped on its large pectoral fins, rocking gently from side to side to mimic the motion of a leaf or seaweed, waiting for its prey. It grows only to 10 cm (4 in) long and, once spotted, it is easily caught.
DEPTH RANGE: 3–40 m+ (9–125 ft+). **DISTRIBUTION:** PNG, Australia, much of the Indo-Pacific. **IDEAL LENS:** 60 mm.

The Leaf Scorpion-fish, like other scorpion-fish, takes on the colouring and patterning of its surroundings. This species can be found in black, white, red, yellow, green, purple or tan.
DEPTH RANGE: 3–40 m+ (9–125 ft+). **DISTRIBUTION:** PNG, Australia, much of the Indo-Pacific. **IDEAL LENS:** 60 mm.

The predatory Leaf Scorpion-fish waits patiently among the coral, dangling a small lure between its eyes to snare prey. Its camouflage fools small fish and other marine animals, such as shrimp. It eats anything that fits in its mouth, which opens much wider than you would imagine.
DEPTH RANGE: 3–40 m+ (9–125 ft+). **DISTRIBUTION:** PNG, Australia, much of the Indo-Pacific. **IDEAL LENS:** 60 mm.

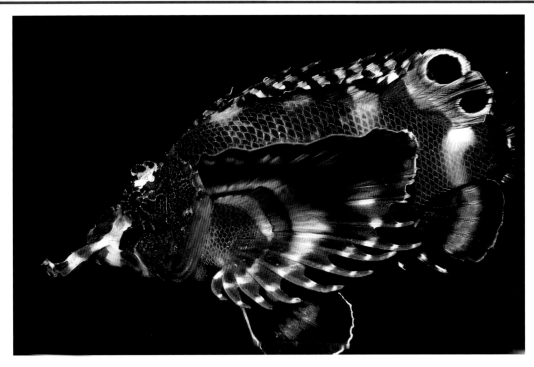

Also known as the Fu-Man-Chu Lionfish because of its large moustache, the small, shy Twin-spot Lionfish (*Dendrochirus biocellatus*) hides in caves and under ledges, and frequents coral reefs and rubble areas.
DEPTH RANGE: 3–25 m (9–80 ft). **DISTRIBUTION:** PNG, Australia, much of the western Pacific. **IDEAL LENS:** 105 mm.

The large, beautiful fins of the Red Firefish (*Pterois volitans*) conceal highly venomous dorsal spines whose stabs can can be extremely painful, even fatal. The deeper the spines penetrate, the more venom enters the victim's body.
DEPTH RANGE: 3–30 m+ (9–100 ft+). **DISTRIBUTION:** PNG, much of the Indo-Pacific, the central Pacific. **IDEAL LENS:** 15–60 mm.

This young adult Red Firefish has yet to fill out and acquire the stronger colouration common to mature fish. As its fins broaden, its unmistakable fish-like outline will becomes less apparent.
DEPTH RANGE: 3–30 m+ (9–100 ft+). DISTRIBUTION: PNG, much of the Indo-Pacific, the central Pacific. IDEAL LENS: 15–60 mm.

The voracious Red Firefish makes use of the reach of its pectoral fins by spreading them out wide to herd and corner prey. Once trapped it will suck its victim down its throat in one piece.
DEPTH RANGE: 3–30 m+ (9–100 ft+). DISTRIBUTION: PNG, much of the Indo-Pacific, the central Pacific. IDEAL LENS: 15–60 mm.

The dramatic Zebra Lionfish (*Dendrochirus zebra*) has large pectoral fins with strands extending past the webbing. Found in caves and crevices on living reefs and drop-offs, and also in rubble areas, this lionfish grows to 20 cm (8 in). (This lionfish is also pictured on page 168.)
DEPTH RANGE: 3–40 m+ (9–125 ft+). DISTRIBUTION: PNG, the central Indo-Pacific. IDEAL LENS: 60 mm.

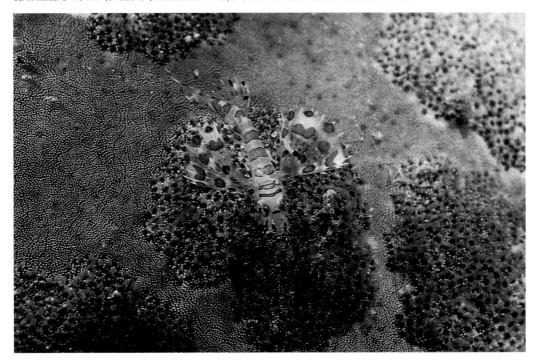

A juvenile Zebra Lionfish rests on a Pincushion Sea Star (*Culcita novaeguineae*). Juveniles often congregate on algae-covered rock outcrops on the sea floor, while adults are more wary, preferring to hide within caves.
DEPTH RANGE: 2 m (6 ft). DISTRIBUTION: PNG. IDEAL LENS: 60 mm.

Most commonly found in shades of red, the Dwarf Lionfish (*Dendrochirus brachypterus*), also known as the Shortfin Turkeyfish, occurs in other colour variations as well. At breeding time both sexes change colour: the males darkening while the females become paler. A shorter pectoral fin distinguishes females from the males.
DEPTH RANGE: 3–40 m+ (9–125 ft+).
DISTRIBUTION: PNG, the central Indo-Pacific.
IDEAL LENS: 60 mm.

This yellow form of the Dwarf Lionfish is unusual and not often seen.
DEPTH RANGE: 3–40 m+ (9–125 ft+).
DISTRIBUTION: PNG, the central Indo-Pacific.
IDEAL LENS: 60 mm.

Dwarf Lionfish tend to keep company with those anemones that inhabit sandy, silty or rubble bottoms.
DEPTH RANGE: 3–40 m+ (9–125 ft+).
DISTRIBUTION: PNG, the central Indo-Pacific.
IDEAL LENS: 60 mm.

The sinister-looking Demon Stinger or Bearded Ghoul (*Inimicus didactylus*) is potentially deadly to humans. It likes sandy weed areas in shallow water near river estuaries. Here it buries itself in the sand with only its head and spines protruding. A number of photographers have been stung, so give this creature a wide berth.
DEPTH RANGE: 1–20 m (3–65 ft). **DISTRIBUTION:** PNG, Australia. **IDEAL LENS:** 60 mm.

Resembling a lumpy, algae-covered rock, the False Stonefish (*Scorpaenopsis diabolus*) waits for a meal. Its hunched back distinguishes it from similar, but far more venomous, large stonefish. (This fish also appears on page 156.)
DEPTH RANGE: 2–25 m (6–80 ft). **DISTRIBUTION:** PNG, much of the Indo-Pacific. **IDEAL LENS:** 60 mm.

The Guam Scorpion-fish (*Scorpaenodes guamensis*) sits on the sea floor awaiting unsuspecting small shrimps and crabs. It hunts mainly at night and favours coral reefs, caves and shipwrecks as habitats.

DEPTH RANGE: 10–40 m+ (35–125 ft+).
DISTRIBUTION: PNG, much of the central Indo-Pacific.
IDEAL LENS: 60 mm.

One of the larger coral reef-dwelling members of the family, growing up to 30 cm (12 in) long, is the Papuan Scorpion-fish (*Scorpaenopsis papuensis*). Individuals from deeper water tend to be reddish, while those from shallower water are often brown or greenish. They are most frequently spotted on outer reef slopes in clear water but live in a variety of habitats.

DEPTH RANGE: 2–40 m+ (6–125 ft+).
DISTRIBUTION: PNG, much of the Indo-Pacific.
IDEAL LENS: 60 mm.

This scorpion-fish is a species of *Scorpaenopsis*. Its pink/brown colouration contrasts with the grey of its background. For an animal whose survival strategy depends so much on camouflage, this individual lays itself vulnerable to predation.

DEPTH RANGE: 2–40 m+ (6–125 ft+).
DISTRIBUTION: PNG, much of the Indo-Pacific.
IDEAL LENS: 60 mm.

To find many species of scorpion-fish, underwater photographers need to study areas thoroughly. Motley colouration and weed-like contours such as found in this species of *Scorpaenopsis* blend so beautifully with the surroundings of reefs that fish are easily missed.
DEPTH RANGE: 2–40 m+ (6–125 ft+).
DISTRIBUTION: PNG, much of the Indo-Pacific.
IDEAL LENS: 60 mm.

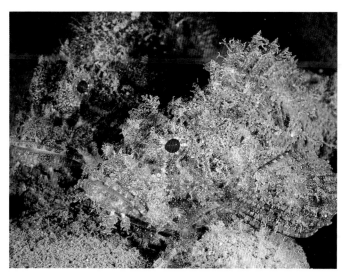

Almost undetectable, these two Spiny-crowned Scorpion-fishes (*Scorpaenopsis* sp.) lurk in the silt and soft sand. They are waiting to snatch their usual prey of small fishes and crustaceans, which they gulp down whole.
DEPTH RANGE: 2–40 m+ (6–125 ft+).
DISTRIBUTION: PNG, much of the Indo-Pacific.
IDEAL LENS: 60 mm.

The filamentous, fleshy growths of this *Scorpaenopsis* scorpion-fish have gone very pale in order to blend with the background.
DEPTH RANGE: 2–40 m+ (6–125 ft+).
DISTRIBUTION: PNG, much of the Indo-Pacific.
IDEAL LENS: 60 mm.

Mimicking a crumpled, dead leaf or a drifting piece of seaweed, the Cockatoo Waspfish (*Ablabys taenianotus*) rocks gently back and forth in the sandy rubble and weed on the bottom of shallow, subtidal areas. Its flattened shape and earthy colour assist in the deception.
DEPTH RANGE: 0.5–15 m (2–50 ft). **DISTRIBUTION:** PNG, much of the **INDO-PACIFIC.** ideal lens: 60 mm.

Cunningly disguised in purple and green to match the Funnel Weed (*Padina gymnospora*) in which it is hiding, this Cockatoo Waspfish takes some looking for. This fish can readily change its colours to blend in with the background.
DEPTH RANGE: 0.5–15 m (2–50 ft). **DISTRIBUTION:** PNG, much of the Indo-Pacific. **IDEAL LENS:** 60 mm.

A small pink fish similar to the Cockatoo Waspfish is the Sailfin Waspfish (*Paracentropogon* sp.). This individual was found on a night dive on a sandy rubble bottom in Milne Bay, Papua New Guinea. Its skin has a shark-skin texture. **DEPTH RANGE:** 5 m (15 ft). **DISTRIBUTION:** PNG. **IDEAL LENS:** 105 mm.

The small, rare 'Bugs Bunny' Scorpion-fish or Ambon Scorpion-fish (*Pteroidichthys amboinensis*) is often very hard to find among the leaves and debris on sandy bottoms where it likes to live. Its long rabbit's ear-like appendages above each eye distinguish it from other species of scorpion-fish.
DEPTH RANGE: 6–40 m+ (20–125 ft+). **DISTRIBUTION:** PNG, Indonesia. **IDEAL LENS:** 60 mm.

Burying itself in soft sand or silt by day and emerging at night to feed, the Blue-eyed Stingfish (*Minous trachy-cephalus*) uses the small claws on its pectoral fins to 'walk' along the bottom. (This fish also appears on page 157.)
DEPTH RANGE: 5–40 m+ (15–125 ft+). **DISTRIBUTION:** PNG, South China Sea, Indonesia–Sri Lanka. **IDEAL LENS:** 60 mm.

CHAPTER 5
ANEMONES AND THEIR RESIDENTS

Anemone fish (or clownfish) and their hosts the anemones have fascinated underwater photographers since submersible cameras were invented. Surprisingly, among the hundreds of species of anemone, only 10 host fish among their toxic tentacles, although their non-toxic undersides provide shelter for small shrimps, crabs and other species of fish. All 10 anemones are found in warm, sunlit tropical waters above 50 m (165 ft). Their tentacles contain nematocysts (stinging cells) used for killing prey and repelling predators, but somehow they do not affect anemone fish. Just how these fish retain immunity remains uncertain. Whatever the truth, the association between these anemones and 'their' fish provides countless photographic opportunities.

Pink Anemone Fish (*Amphiprion perideraion*) among tentacles of the Magnificent Sea Anemone (*Heteractis magnifica*). **DEPTH RANGE:** 3–20 m (9–65 ft). **DISTRIBUTION:** PNG, much of central Indo-Pacific. **IDEAL LENS:** 60–105 mm.

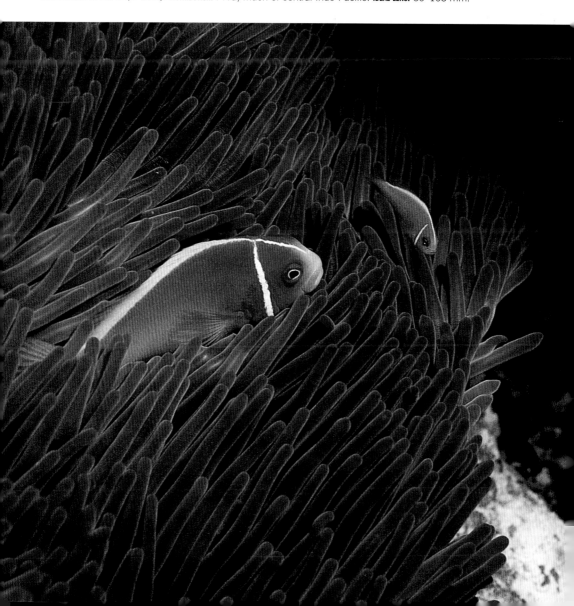

Often found in groups of three or more in the one anemone, the Orange Anemone Fish (*Amphiprion sandaracinos*) is usually found in association with Mertens' Sea Anemone (*Stichodactyla mertensii*).
DEPTH RANGE: 6–20 m (20–65 ft).
DISTRIBUTION: PNG, Indonesia, Australia, Philippines.
IDEAL LENS: 60–105 mm.

The Clown Anemone Fish (*Amphiprion percula*) looks very much like its relative the False Clown Anemone Fish (*A. ocellaris*), except that it has 10 dorsal spines, not 11, and its front dorsal fin is shorter.
DEPTH RANGE: 3–20 m (9–65 ft).
DISTRIBUTION: PNG, Indonesia, Australia, Philippines.
IDEAL LENS: 60–105 mm.

Clark's Anemone Fish (*Amphiprion clarkii*) is seen here among the tentacles of the Leathery Sea Anemone (*Heteractis crispa*). Common in most habitats, it is also found in association with several other large anemones, including the Adhesive Sea Anemone (*Cryptodendrum adhaesivum*) and the Magnificent Sea Anemone (*H. magnifica*).
DEPTH RANGE: 3–20 m (9–65 ft).
DISTRIBUTION: PNG, much of the Indo-Pacific.
IDEAL LENS: 60 mm.

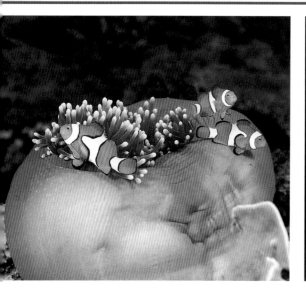

This Magnificent Sea Anemone (*Heteractis magnifica*) has retracted its tentacles, leaving these Clown Anemonefish (*Amphiprion percula*) vulnerable to predators. Anemones on reef-tops may partially retract their tentacles in order to digest food.
DEPTH RANGE: 2–25 m (6–75 ft).
DISTRIBUTION: PNG, throughout the Indo-Pacific.
IDEAL LENS: 24–60 mm.

Coming in two colour forms, the Saddleback Anemone Fish (*Amphiprion polymnus*) is usually black and white. Found in sheltered waters with soft sandy bottoms, it associates mainly with Haddon's Sea Anemone (*Stichodactyla haddoni*).
DEPTH RANGE: 3–30 m (9–100 ft).
DISTRIBUTION: PNG, much of the central Indo-Pacific.
IDEAL LENS: 60–105 mm.

The White-bonnet Anemone Fish (*Amphiprion leucokranos*) is thought to be a hybrid between the Orange-fin Anemone Fish (*A. chrysopterus*) and the Orange Anemone Fish (*A. sandaracinos*). It is usually found singly in the company of Orange-fin Anemone Fish but occasionally two or even three fish are found in the one anemone.
DEPTH RANGE: 2–20 m (6–65 ft).
DISTRIBUTION: PNG and the Solomon Islands.
IDEAL LENS: 60–105 mm.

Able to change costume at short notice, the white bands of the Spinecheek Anemone Fish (*Premnas biaculeatus*) can quickly darken to an almost black colour. This fish gets its name from the single spine on each cheek, which, in an adult, projects over the first white band.
DEPTH RANGE: 3–20 m (9–65 ft).
DISTRIBUTION: PNG.
IDEAL LENS: 60–105 mm.

Startled by an approaching diver, this yellow-and-black Saddleback Anemone Fish quickly buries itself down the throat of its host, Haddon's Sea Anemone. The tail of a second fish is just protruding. The more common black-and-white form of this fish is pictured opposite.
DEPTH RANGE: 8 m (25 ft).
DISTRIBUTION: PNG.
IDEAL LENS: 60 mm.

Orange, black, yellow — and two almost fluorescent blue bands — make the Orange-fin Anemone Fish startling. It has immunity among six different anemones, including the Leathery Sea Anemone (*Heteractis crispa*), the Magnificent Sea Anemone and Haddon's Sea Anemone.
DEPTH RANGE: 3–15 m (9–50 ft).
DISTRIBUTION: PNG and the western Pacific.
IDEAL LENS: 60–105 mm.

From time to time water temperatures rise. If the water stays warm for some time, it is well known that some corals become bleached — so also do some anemones. In this case the Spinecheek Anemone Fish, sheltering on the Bulb-tentacle Sea Anemone (*Entacmaea quadricolor*), has gone white.
DEPTH RANGE: 4 m (12 ft).
DISTRIBUTION: PNG.
IDEAL LENS: 60 mm.

This Clark's Anemone Fish (*Amphiprion clarkii*) is maintaining a vigil over its mat of reddish orange eggs while remaining undercover within the tentacles of its host, Haddon's Sea Anemone (*Stichodactyla haddoni*).
DEPTH RANGE: 2–30 m (5–100 ft). DISTRIBUTION: PNG and the Indo-Pacific. IDEAL LENS: 20-24 mm.

Anemone fish lay their eggs beside their host anemone, mostly on stones. Fish of sand-dwelling anemones will drag hard objects, including sticks, alongside the anemone to provide a laying surface. Here the eggs of the Clown Anemone Fish (*Amphiprion percula*) are so close up that you can just see the eyes of the fish within the eggs.
DEPTH RANGE: 2–30 m (5–100 ft). **DISTRIBUTION:** PNG, throughout the Indo-Pacific. **IDEAL LENS:** 105 mm + 4 dioptre.

Using the anenome's mass of tentacles as a shelter from predatory fish, the anemone crab *Neopetrolisthes ohshimai* filters plankton from the water. Like anemone fish, it is impervious to the toxins produced by its host.
DEPTH RANGE: 3–25 m (9–80 ft) **DISTRIBUTION:** PNG, much of the Indo-Pacific. **IDEAL LENS:** 105 mm.

CHAPTER 6
SANDY WEED AND RUBBLE ZONES

Sandy weed zones, populated by a multiplicity of seagrasses and algae, are rich in photographic opportunity. Along fringing coastlines and in sheltered lagoons, sandy weed zones occur wherever sand movement is minimal. Rubble zones — areas where dead coral broken by wave action accumulates — at first glance seem devoid of life but rubble zones often grade into areas alive with algae and seagrasses and so creatures often migrate there. Both zones are important nursery grounds for many sand-dwellers and young fish, molluscs, crustaceans and cephalopods hide among the seaweeds or dart beneath the rubble. Predators are relatively few because there are bigger pickings elsewhere. This chapter reveals just some of the huge variety of life-forms making a living in these little-explored habitats. Diving by day or night will produce great results but night dives are especially rewarding because many marine creatures are nocturnal.

This photograph was taken at night as this mollusc, a species of sundial from the genus *Architectonica*, only emerges from its daytime hideaway beneath sand to forage come dusk.
DEPTH RANGE: 5–20 m (15–65 ft).
DISTRIBUTION: PNG, Indonesia.
IDEAL LENS: 60 mm.

Striking fear into the hearts of small molluscs, moon snails are formidable predators. They hunt down small snails, drill into the shell and suck out the helpless victim. Here the moon snail *Neverita didyma* is searching for a meal.
DEPTH RANGE: 2–40 m (6–125 ft).
DISTRIBUTION: PNG, most of the Indo-Pacific.
IDEAL LENS: 60 mm.

Moon snails leave a furrowed trail as they plough over or just below a sandy surface and often rest in a small hump of sand at the end of the trail. This species of *Natica* is revealed scraping away surrounding sand.
DEPTH RANGE: 2–30 m (6–100 ft).
DISTRIBUTION: PNG.
IDEAL LENS: 60 mm.

Looking for all the world like a fancy cream cake from a French patisserie, the nocturnal moon snail *Tanea undulata* cruises the sea floor foraging in the soft sand silt for tasty morsels.
DEPTH RANGE: 5–40 m (15–125 ft).
DISTRIBUTION: PNG, Philippines, Indonesia, Australia.
IDEAL LENS: 60 mm.

OPPOSITE: The nocturnal moon snail *Niticarius orientalis* is found in the clear water of sandy silt areas.
DEPTH RANGE: 5–30 m (15–100 ft). **DISTRIBUTION:** PNG, the central Indo-Pacific. **IDEAL LENS:** 60 mm.

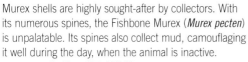

Murex shells are highly sought-after by collectors. With its numerous spines, the Fishbone Murex (*Murex pecten*) is unpalatable. Its spines also collect mud, camouflaging it well during the day, when the animal is inactive.
DEPTH RANGE: 5–40 m (15–125 ft).
DISTRIBUTION: PNG, throughout the Indo-Pacific.
IDEAL LENS: 60 mm.

The murex *Haustellum haustellum* carries the characteristic shell shape but without the spines. It remains buried during the day in sandy silt bottoms and emerges at night to feed.
DEPTH RANGE: 5–20 m (15–65 ft).
DISTRIBUTION: PNG, throughout the Indo-Pacific.
IDEAL LENS: 60 mm.

Helmet shells are sand-burrowing carnivores. This adult *Phalium* (*Semicassis*) *bisulcatum* is found in soft sand and seaweed areas.
DEPTH RANGE: 3–40 m+ (9–125 ft+).
DISTRIBUTION: PNG, Indonesia, Australia.
IDEAL LENS: 60 mm.

This is the juvenile helmet shell of *Phalium* (*Semicassis*) *bisulcatum* out foraging by night. Helmet shells are surprisingly fond of sea urchins.
DEPTH RANGE: 3–40 m+ (9–125 ft+).
DISTRIBUTION: PNG, Indonesia, Australia.
IDEAL LENS: 60 mm.

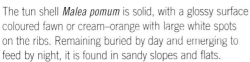

The tun shell *Malea pomum* is solid, with a glossy surface coloured fawn or cream–orange with large white spots on the ribs. Remaining buried by day and emerging to feed by night, it is found in sandy slopes and flats.
DEPTH RANGE: 3–20 m (9–65 ft).
DISTRIBUTION: PNG, Australia, Solomon Islands.
IDEAL LENS: 24–60 mm.

This is a juvenile helmet shell from the genus *Phalium* out on the prowl. At this stage its shell is extremely thin-walled and very easily broken, making it an easy meal for predators.
DEPTH RANGE: 3–25 m (9–80 ft).
DISTRIBUTION: PNG, Philippines.
IDEAL LENS: 60 mm.

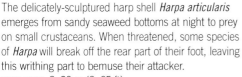

The delicately-sculptured harp shell *Harpa articularis* emerges from sandy seaweed bottoms at night to prey on small crustaceans. When threatened, some species of *Harpa* will break off the rear part of their foot, leaving this writhing part to bemuse their attacker.
DEPTH RANGE: 3–20 m (9–65 ft).
DISTRIBUTION: PNG, Australia, Philippines, Solomon Islands.
IDEAL LENS: 60 mm.

The commonly-occurring fig shell, *Ficus subintermedia*, creeps along sea floors of sand, silt or finely-broken rubble. Fig shells are active creatures. Undeterred by ferocious spines, they like to feed on sea urchins or other echinoderms.
DEPTH RANGE: 4–25 m (12–80 ft).
DISTRIBUTION: PNG, most of the Indo-Pacific.
IDEAL LENS: 60 mm.

Like other molluscs, the baler shell *Melo broderipii* frequently buries itself as the tidal waters fall, emerging at night to feed on sandy silt bottoms. This shell can also be found on open reefs where there is a lot of sand. Indigenous Australians used baler shells as ready-made containers, perfectly-shaped for bailing water from canoes; hence the name of the shell.

DEPTH RANGE: 3–20 m (9–65 ft).
DISTRIBUTION: PNG, Australia, Indonesia.
IDEAL LENS: 24 mm.

During the day the trumpet shell *Cymatium gutturnium* remains buried under the sand. By night it crawls along the bottom in search of food. Its shell is very thick and solid and the extension of its shell acts as a snorkel when the creature lies buried beneath the sand.

DEPTH RANGE: 3–25 m (9–80 ft).
DISTRIBUTION: PNG, Australia, Indonesia, Japan.
IDEAL LENS: 60 mm.

Here you see a cowry's unmistakable smooth shiny shell with its subtle speckled blotches. This pretty Humphrey's Cowry (*Cypraea humphreysii*) is often found on debris such as logs or old wharf piles in seagrass or rubble areas.

DEPTH RANGE: 2–10 m (6–35 ft).
DISTRIBUTION: PNG, Australia, Solomon Islands–Fiji.
IDEAL LENS: 60 mm.

The deadly Textile Cone (*Conus textile*) uses its powerful neurotoxins not only to subdue prey, but also to avoid predation. A number of people have died after receiving poisonous darts from this species.
DEPTH RANGE: 0–10 m (0–35 ft).
DISTRIBUTION: PNG, the tropical Indo-Pacific.
IDEAL LENS: 60 mm.

Equally dangerous is the Geography Cone (*Conus geographus*). It is the largest cone of the Indo-Pacific, sometimes exceeding 15 cm (6 in) long, and it feeds on small fishes or other molluscs, mainly at night.
DEPTH RANGE: 0–10 m (0–35 ft).
DISTRIBUTION: PNG, the tropical Indo-Pacific.
IDEAL LENS: 24–60 mm.

With its shell sometimes obscured by a growth of algae, the strom *Strombus aurisdianae* may be difficult to spot. It is usually found feeding on algae or detritus in sandy areas or areas with very short seagrass.
DEPTH RANGE: 2–10 m (6–35 ft).
DISTRIBUTION: PNG, most of the Indo-Pacific.
IDEAL LENS: 60 mm.

Turris crispa is a large turrid, commonly found on sandy to silty bottoms. Although it feeds both by day and night, it spends the vast majority of its time buried within the substrate.
DEPTH RANGE: 2–40 m+ (6–125 ft+).
DISTRIBUTION: PNG, most of the Indo-Pacific.
IDEAL LENS: 60 mm.

The pretty Rose Petal Bubble Shell (*Hydatina physis*) is actually a sea slug which spends much of its time beneath the sand, although it is known to feed both day and night. In warmer months it spawns in shallow water, issuing creamy white ruffles that contain strings of tiny eggs.
DEPTH RANGE: 1–20 m (3–65 ft).
DISTRIBUTION: PNG, throughout the Indo-Pacific.
IDEAL LENS: 60 mm.

The bubble shell *Micromelo undata* is another sea slug that spends most of its time buried beneath the sand. Its very fragile shell is only tiny and cannot possibly accommodate the entire animal. It does, however, have room to house and protect the animal's vital organs.
DEPTH RANGE: 1–20 m (3–65 ft).
DISTRIBUTION: PNG, throughout the Indo-Pacific.
IDEAL LENS: 60 mm.

The very powerful Crocodile Snake Eel (*Brachysomophis crocodilinus*) is found in soft sandy to small pebbly bottoms with only 10–15 cm (4–6 in) of its head poking up from the sea floor.
DEPTH RANGE: 3–20 m (9–65 ft).
DISTRIBUTION: PNG, Indonesia, Solomon Islands, Australia.
IDEAL LENS: 60 mm.

Not to be mistaken for the Striped Snake Eel, which looks similar, the very active Spotted Snake Eel (*Myrichthys maculosus*) can often be seen hunting around rubble areas.
DEPTH RANGE: 3–20 m (9–65 ft).
DISTRIBUTION: PNG, much of the Indo-Pacific.
IDEAL LENS: 24 mm.

Found in soft sand areas or seaweed beds, Marbled Snake Eels (*Callechelys marmorata*) are usually seen only as here, with a few centimetres of the head protruding from the bottom.
DEPTH RANGE: 2–20 m (6–65 ft).
DISTRIBUTION: PNG, Australia.
IDEAL LENS: 60 mm.

The Clown Snake Eel (*Ophichthus bonaparti*), which inhabits soft sandy bottoms, is often seen with only the head protruding from the sand. When disturbed they disappear completely below the sand.
DEPTH RANGE: 3–25 m (9–80 ft).
DISTRIBUTION: PNG, Indonesia, Philippines.
IDEAL LENS: 60 mm.

The Stargazer Snake Eel (*Brachysomophis cirrocheilos*) can be found living in soft grey–black sandy silt areas, usually in still bays near estuaries. Note the very impressive row of teeth.

DEPTH RANGE: 3–25 m (9–80 ft).
DISTRIBUTION: PNG.
IDEAL LENS: 60 mm.

The bobbit worm (*Eunice* sp.) spends most of its time buried in sand or silt. When searching for food, it rises 10–15 cm (4–6 in) or so out of its hiding place to ensnare a passing fish or crustacean, then disappears beneath the sand to digest it. Each year hundreds of thousands of sexually-mature bobbit worms gather for a frenzy of fertilisation. With their eggs and sperm concentrated in their tail segments, their tails detach and float to the surface, forming a thick soup of writhing, headless worms.

DEPTH RANGE: 3–20 m (9–65 ft).
DISTRIBUTION: PNG, Indonesia.
IDEAL LENS: 60 mm.

Like a whorl of wispy filaments on a stick, sea pens have a primary polyp as the 'stalk' and rows of secondary polyps for capturing food. These polyps also pump water through a series of canals thereby allowing the colony to extend upright to feed and to contract into the sandy silt bottom. The specimen pictured here, a species of the genus *Veretillum*, was found on a night dive. The pink–red stem with white polyps stands out against the dark background.

DEPTH RANGE: 4 m (12 ft).
DISTRIBUTION: PNG.
IDEAL LENS: 60 mm.

Many sea pens luminesce when touched, often radiating coloured pulses of light. Found on a night-time dive, this specimen from the genus *Scytalium* has a much stockier build than the sea pen *Veretillum* and a tighter arrangement of secondary polyps.
DEPTH RANGE: 6 m (20 ft).
DISTRIBUTION: PNG.
IDEAL LENS: 60 mm.

Found on the same night-time dive upon a sandy rubble bottom was this sand anemone from the genus *Actiniaria*.
DEPTH RANGE: 5 m (15 ft).
DISTRIBUTION: PNG.
IDEAL LENS: 60 mm.

Another tropical beauty is the rather startling sand anemone from the genus *Condylactis*. It has a green centre with almost iridescent blue ends on its smooth arms and is found upon rubble bottoms.
DEPTH RANGE: 4–20 m (12–65 ft).
DISTRIBUTION: PNG, Micronesia.
IDEAL LENS: 60 mm.

Sea pens, like this species from the genus *Virgularia*, retreat into the sand if they are under threat. They are usually found on sandy slopes or in sandy areas at the base of drop-offs. Close examination of many sea pen species reveals a variety of smaller creatures hidden within their delicate branches.

DEPTH RANGE: 5–40 m+ (15–125 ft+). **DISTRIBUTION:** PNG. **IDEAL LENS:** 60 mm.

This small, almost completely transparent shrimp from the genus *Periclimenes* is grazing its way along the branches of a sea pen. These vulnerable shrimps find it safest to venture out only at night.
DEPTH RANGE: 6 m (20 ft). **DISTRIBUTION:** PNG. **IDEAL LENS:** 105 mm.

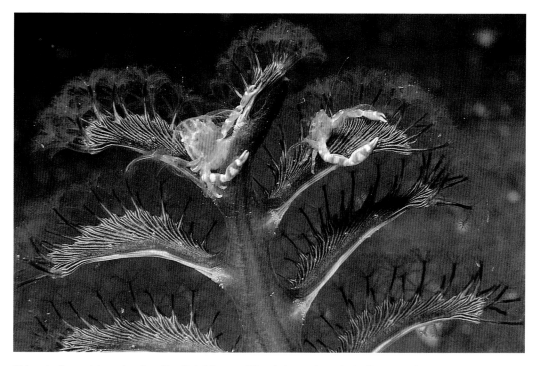

This pair of porcelain crabs, *Porcellanella triloba*, are sifting their way through the filaments of this unknown sea pen in search of tasty morsels. It is common for a male and female to take up residence on the one host.
DEPTH RANGE: 5–40 m+ (15–125 ft+). **DISTRIBUTION:** PNG, Australia, Indonesia. **IDEAL LENS:** 105 mm.

The Fire Urchin (*Asthenosoma varium*) is found in locations varying from sandy rubble bottoms to rocky slopes. Its prickly nature may seem like an uncomfortable place to lodge but, despite the stinging spines loaded with toxins, small animals do use this host for protection and enticing food particles are often caught among the spines. Never touch this urchin as these spines are extremely painful to humans. (The Fire Urchin is also pictured on pages 111 and 135).

DEPTH RANGE: 5–40 m (15–125 ft). DISTRIBUTION: PNG, Indonesia, most of the Indo-Pacific. IDEAL LENS: 24 mm.

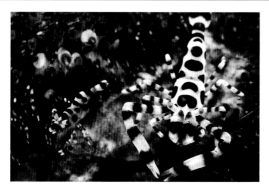

Taking good care to choose a spot free of spines, pairs of Coleman's Shrimp (*Periclimenes colemani*) often sit on Fire Urchins. The female is always larger than the male.
DEPTH RANGE: 5–40 m (15–125 ft+).
DISTRIBUTION: PNG, Indonesia, Australia. **IDEAL LENS:** 105 mm.

Nothing on the reef is straightforward. Here you see a colour variation of Coleman's Shrimp.
DEPTH RANGE: 5–40 m (15–125 ft+).
DISTRIBUTION: PNG, Indonesia, Australia.
IDEAL LENS: 105 mm.

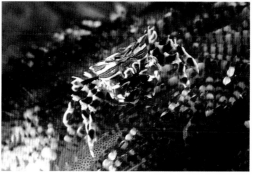

This colourful shrimp, *Allopontonia iaini*, lives at the Fire Urchin's base where it takes a ride, gathering food from the sea floor as the urchin moves along.
DEPTH RANGE: 5–40 m (15–125 ft).
DISTRIBUTION: PNG, most of the Indo-Pacific region.
IDEAL LENS: 105 mm.

Also grazing along the sea floor as it piggybacks on the Fire Urchin is the tiny Adam's Crab (*Zebrida adamsii*). (This crab is also pictured on page 134.)
DEPTH RANGE: 5–20 m (15–65 ft).
DISTRIBUTION: PNG, much of the central Indo-Pacific.
IDEAL LENS: 60–105 mm.

Undeterred by the urchin's spines, the small parasitic snail, *Luetzenia asthenosomae* makes a meal of its host, the Fire Urchin, by feeding on its body fluids. This snail is often seen in small colonies with trails of eggs.
DEPTH RANGE: 5–40 m (15–125 ft).
DISTRIBUTION: PNG, Indonesia, Australia.
IDEAL LENS: 105 mm.

Unlike sea anemones, tube anemones live within a strong, flexible tube of sand-encrusted mucous. These tubes are sometimes buried completely below the sea floor, but more often they protrude a little above the surface as in this species from the genus *Cerianthus*. Usually found in areas of sand or silt and hosting a number of creatures, a tube anemone can quickly retract into its tube if threatened.

DEPTH RANGE: 3 m+ (9 ft+). **DISTRIBUTION:** PNG, most of the Indo-Pacific. **IDEAL LENS:** 20–60 mm.

Pictured here sheltering in the hidey-hole provided by its host, the colourful anemone crab *Lissocarcinus laevis* inhabits the trunk of the *Cerianthus* tube anemone until threatened or until the anemone retracts its tentacles.
DEPTH RANGE: 5–20 m (15–65 ft). **DISTRIBUTION:** PNG, throughout the Indo-Pacific. **IDEAL LENS:** 60–105 mm.

Sheltered by a tube anemone (*Cerianthus* species), the beautifully-patterned shrimp *Thor amboinensis* can be found in pairs or whole colonies on many anemones, scuttling inside when the anemone retracts its tentacles.
DEPTH RANGE: 3–20 m (9–65 ft). **DISTRIBUTION:** PNG, the Indo-Pacific. **IDEAL LENS:** 105 mm.

With its bloom of waving tentacle-like polyps, this mushroom coral *Heliofungia actiniformis* could easily be mistaken for an anemone but it is in fact a hard coral because its tissues are studded with calcium carbonate spicules. Often found on live reefs as well as rubble bottoms, mushroom corals host many small creatures.

DEPTH RANGE: 3–20 m (9–65 ft). **DISTRIBUTION:** PNG, Australia, Solomon Islands, Indonesia. **IDEAL LENS:** 15–24 mm.

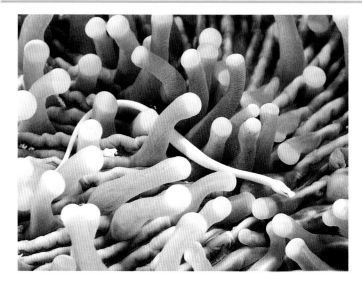

Small, white and eel-like, the Coral Pipefish (*Siokunichthys nigrolineatus*) will often insinuate itself among the polyps of mushroom corals.
DEPTH RANGE: 3–20 m (9–65 ft).
DISTRIBUTION: PNG, Australia, Solomon Islands, Philippines.
IDEAL LENS: 60 mm.

A denizen of the mushroom coral *Heliofungia actiniformis*, the Eggshell Shrimp (*Hamodactylus corallicola*), has a clear body with two white caps that mimic the tips of the coral's polyps.
DEPTH RANGE: 3–20 m (9–65 ft).
DISTRIBUTION: PNG, Australia, Solomon Islands, Philippines.
IDEAL LENS: 105 mm.

The Mushroom Coral Shrimp (*Periclimenes kororensis*) is found only on mushroom corals, in this case *Heliofungia actiniformis*. Its white 'bonnet' mimics the white tips of the coral so that, despite its red body, it blends in from above where predators are likely to lurk.
DEPTH RANGE: 3–20 m (9–65 ft).
DISTRIBUTION: PNG, Australia, Solomon Islands, Philippines.
IDEAL LENS: 105 mm.

One of the major commercial prawn species, the Western King Prawn (*Penaeus latisulcatus*) buries itself in the sand or silt during the day when it would be easy prey for larger creatures, only emerging at night to feed. This shrimp inhabits sandy silt and seagrass areas and can grow up to 300 mm long.

DEPTH RANGE: 5–25 m (15–80 ft).
DISTRIBUTION: PNG, Indonesia, Australia.
IDEAL LENS: 60 mm.

While still caught commercially, Coral Prawns (*Metapenaeopsis* sp.) attract lower prices than Penaeus species since they are considerably smaller, growing to no more than 25 mm long. Found in sand and rubble areas, they, too, are nocturnal.

DEPTH RANGE: 2–20 m (6–65 ft).
DISTRIBUTION: PNG, Australia, Philippines.
IDEAL LENS: 60 mm.

Mantis shrimps are formidable predators of other crustaceans, small fish, molluscs and worms. Their strong claws are used to break the shell of their prey. Mantis shrimps are actually very large prawns, up to 30 cm long. Most display brilliant iridescent blues and greens but this rather drab shrimp of the genus *Lysiosquilla* usually lives in soft sandy or silty bottoms in relatively still waters and prefers to remain camouflaged.

DEPTH RANGE: 5–15 m (15–50 ft).
DISTRIBUTION: PNG.
IDEAL LENS: 60 mm.

This bright orange shrimp species of the genus *Lysiosquilla* stands out against a dark background. Rarely seen away from its hole, it keeps well hidden, buried in the sand and rubble of the sea floor.
DEPTH RANGE: 5–15 m (15–50 ft).
DISTRIBUTION: PNG.
IDEAL LENS: 60 mm.

Mantis shrimps from the genus *Lysiosquilla* lie hidden in the soft substrate and make lightning strikes, extending their strong claws to grab their prey before retreating back into the sand to eat it.
DEPTH RANGE: 5–10 m (15–35 ft).
DISTRIBUTION: PNG, Solomon Islands, Indonesia, Australia.
IDEAL LENS: 60 mm.

The mantis shrimp *Odontodactylus scyllarus* is probably the most colourful of all the mantis shrimps and this individual displays all the colours of the rainbow. It inhabits rocky reefs and rubble areas and, like other mantis shrimps, is often seen shuffling across the bottom or suddenly seeking refuge in its burrow.
DEPTH RANGE: 3–20 m (9–65 ft).
DISTRIBUTION: PNG, Solomon Islands, Indonesia, Australia.
IDEAL LENS: 60–105 mm.

This small mantis shrimp (*Odontodactylus brevirostris*) was found feeding on small molluscs among the leaves and silt at a river mouth in Milne Bay, Papua New Guinea. Presumably the prospects of a molluscan feast outweighed the risks of being exposed to equally hungry predators.
DEPTH RANGE: 3–10 m (9–35 ft).
DISTRIBUTION: PNG, Solomon Islands, Indonesia, Australia.
IDEAL LENS: 105 mm.

Although short-spined and pretty the Flower Urchin (*Toxopneustes pileolus*) is nonetheless extremely dangerous. These urchins should not be handled, as fatalities have been recorded. Found in sandy rubble to seaweed flats, it lies buried under the sand by day emerging at night to feed. Its colours vary from white to brown to pink.
DEPTH RANGE: 3–15 m (9–50 ft). **DISTRIBUTION:** PNG, throughout the Indo-Pacific. **IDEAL LENS:** 105 mm.

Here, the venomous toothed discs of the Flower Urchin are shown clearly. These discs, called pedicellariae, cover the entire animal and can easily break off in the soft skin between a person's fingers.
DEPTH RANGE: 3–15 m (9–50 ft). **DISTRIBUTION:** PNG, throughout the Indo-Pacific. **IDEAL LENS:** 105 mm.

A common inhabitant of the sandy weed and rubble zones are the *Porites* corals and upon these live Christmas-tree Worms (*Spirobranchus giganteus*). These worms shelter permanently in their tubes with only the feathery tentacles poking out to feed on planktonic creatures floating or swimming through the water column. Being very sensitive to changes in light and pressure, the tentacles quickly retract if disturbed. (Christmas-tree Worms are also pictured on pages 31 and 169.)

DEPTH RANGE: 4 m (12 ft). **DISTRIBUTION:** PNG. **IDEAL LENS:** 60 mm.

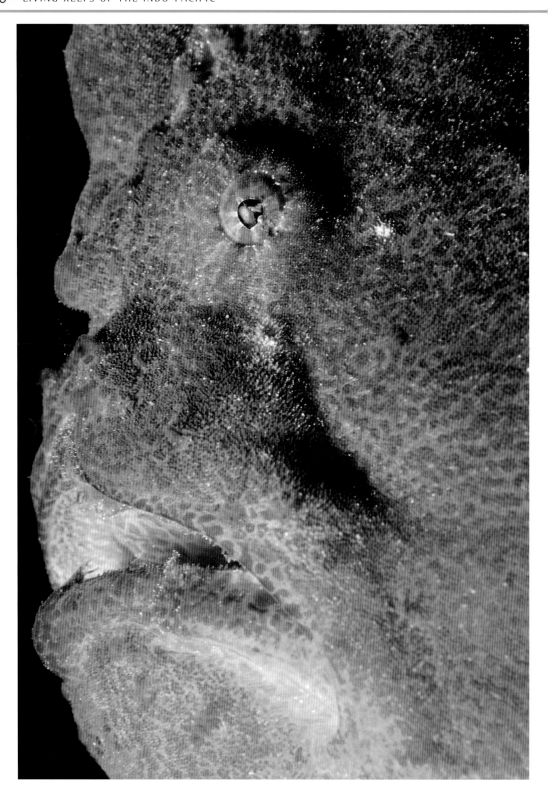

This close-up of the face of the Giant Anglerfish (*Antennarius commersonii*) shows details only another anglerfish could love. This specimen was over 30 cm (12 in) long.

DEPTH RANGE: 5 m (15 ft). **DISTRIBUTION:** PNG, much of the Indo-Pacific. **IDEAL LENS:** 60 mm.

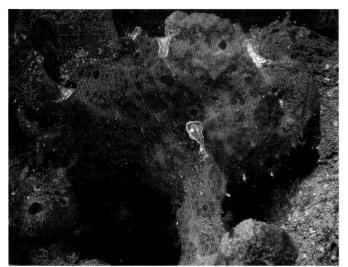

Easily outgrowing similar species, adult Giant Anglerfish grow to 30 cm long. An inhabitant of reefs and sand areas, this fish often mimics the red–maroon sponge on which it is found. Specimens have been observed in almost the same location for up to eight months at a time.
DEPTH RANGE: 5–30 m (15–100 ft).
DISTRIBUTION: PNG, Indonesia, northern Australia, most of the Indo-Pacific.
IDEAL LENS: 60–105 mm.

A colour variant of a Giant Anglerfish lies in wait within a meadow of seagrass. When a curious creature of suitable size comes to investigate further it will be sucked up whole in a split second.
DEPTH RANGE: 3 m (9 ft).
DISTRIBUTION: PNG, most of the Indo-Pacific.
IDEAL LENS: 105 mm.

Somewhat out of place on a rubble bottom, Sargassum Anglerfish (*Histrio histrio*) are usually found on rafts of sargassum weed (*Sargassum* sp.), along with eggs and juveniles. To escape from predators, it can leap out of the water onto these rafts, remaining there for some time before returning to the water. (The Sargassum Anglerfish can also be seen on page 131.)
DEPTH RANGE: Surface.
DISTRIBUTION: PNG, all tropical Indo-Pacific except the eastern Pacific.
IDEAL LENS: 60 mm.

The Painted Anglerfish (*Antennarius pictus*) are found in an array of colours and patterns. They frequent sponge habitats and choose colours that blend with their own.
DEPTH RANGE: 3–20 m (9–65 ft). **DISTRIBUTION:** PNG, Indonesia, Solomon Islands, Australia. **IDEAL LENS:** 105 mm.

The yellow form of the Painted Anglerfish is often found in association with a small yellow sponge on the sea floor. Colour matching with its habitat greatly facilitates the anglerfish's ambushing strategies.
DEPTH RANGE: 3–20 m (9–65 ft). **DISTRIBUTION:** PNG, Indonesia, Solomon Islands, Australia. **IDEAL LENS:** 105 mm.

This specimen of the Painted Anglerfish was found on a sandy rubble bottom living among sponges of the genus *Dysidea*. Its extendible mouth and expandable stomach can accommodate surprisingly large prey.
DEPTH RANGE: 5–30 m (15–20 ft).
DISTRIBUTION: PNG, most of the Indo-Pacific.
IDEAL LENS: 105 mm.

Pictured here is another colour variation of the Painted Anglerfish. When diving among sandy weed and rubble zones it is always worth carefully examining sponges to see if you can spot anglerfish.
DEPTH RANGE: 5–30 m (15–20 ft).
DISTRIBUTION: PNG, most of the Indo-Pacific.
IDEAL LENS: 105 mm.

Given that there are small black sponges on coral reefs, it is not surprising that the chameleon-like Painted Anglerfish is also found in a black colour variation.
DEPTH RANGE: 5–30 m (15–20 ft).
DISTRIBUTION: PNG, most of the Indo-Pacific.
IDEAL LENS: 105 mm.

The Painted Anglerfish (*Antennarius pictus*) is clearly not built for speed but there's more than one way to catch a fish.
DEPTH RANGE: 5–30 m (15–100 ft).
DISTRIBUTION: PNG, most of the Indo-Pacific.
IDEAL LENS: 105 mm.

This is another colour variation of the Painted Anglerfish. Looking for all the world like part of the scenery, its patience and vigilance will doubtless pay off.
DEPTH RANGE: 5–30 m (15–100 ft).
DISTRIBUTION: PNG, most of the Indo-Pacific.
IDEAL LENS: 105 mm.

This is a particularly subtle colour variation of the Painted Anglerfish. Found within the shallows, this individual is trying to mimic the Green Urn Ascidian (*Didemnum molle*).
DEPTH RANGE: 5–30 m (15–100 ft).
DISTRIBUTION: PNG, most of the Indo-Pacific.
IDEAL LENS: 105 mm.

The Clown Anglerfish (*Antennarius maculatus*) stands out on a rubble bottom, its 'lure' resembling a small fish, but on vertical rock faces with short filamentous algae it is less obvious. Adults develop wart-like swellings.
DEPTH RANGE: 5–30 m (15–100 ft).
DISTRIBUTION: PNG, most of the central Indo-Pacific.
IDEAL LENS: 105 mm.

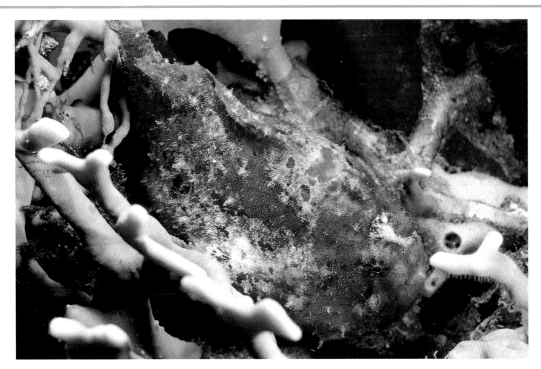

This Scarlet Anglerfish (*Antennarius coccineus*) was photographed in Milne Bay, Papua New Guinea, lurking among fire coral under an old jetty. Jetties and their debris often provide good habitats for these fish.
DEPTH RANGE: 5–30 m (15–100 ft). **DISTRIBUTION:** Most of the Indo-Pacific. **IDEAL LENS:** 105 mm.

Easily identified by the large, dark spot on its dorsal fin, the Spotfin Anglerfish (*Antennarius nummifer*) is highly variable in body colour. This fish lurks around reefs and on rubble bottoms, feeding on small fish or crustaceans.
DEPTH RANGE: 6–40 m (20–125 ft). **DISTRIBUTION:** PNG, most of the Indo-Pacific. **IDEAL LENS:** 60 mm.

Some call it home, others dinner — coralline algae such as *Halimeda macroloba* pictured here host a variety of creatures. The semi-rigid branches reach into the water column, supported by 'skeletons' of calcium carbonate. Exfoliated flakes of dead 'skeletons' form a characteristic sediment on many reefs. Coralline algae are common in still waters on fringing reefs, in bays and lagoons, on sandy rubble and silty seabeds.

DEPTH RANGE: 3–20 m (9–65 ft). **DISTRIBUTION:** PNG, much of the Indo-Pacific. **IDEAL LENS:** 60–24 mm.

As its name suggests, the Many-host Goby (*Pleurosicya mossambica*) is able to benefit from associating with a variety of hosts. Here a semi-transparent goby is lingering by the lobed filaments of Halimeda macroloba. Other hosts may include coloured sponges, ascidians, soft corals, molluscs and sea cucumbers. These gobies can vary in colour from semi-transparent to pale pink, yellow or green.
DEPTH RANGE: 3–10 m (9–35 ft).
DISTRIBUTION: PNG, much of the Indo-Pacific.
IDEAL LENS: 105 mm.

Easily undetected in its habitat, the small sea slug *Elysia pusilla* is found only on calcareous algae, using them as both a food source and a breeding ground.
DEPTH RANGE: 2–20 m (6–65 ft).
DISTRIBUTION: PNG, the central Indo-Pacific.
IDEAL LENS: 105 mm.

By adding a piece of *Halimeda macroloba* above its head the Halimeda Crab (*Huenia heraldica*) is completely disguised. The ability of this crab to 'disappear' on its algal host renders it invisible to predators. (This Halimeda Crab is also pictured on page 129.)
DEPTH RANGE: 3–20 m (9–65 ft).
DISTRIBUTION: PNG, Australia.
IDEAL LENS: 105 mm.

The coralline alga *Halimeda cylindracea* plays host to many marine animals. Its seemingly chaotic architecture makes for a maze of hiding and feeding crooks and crannies. It is usually found on fringing reefs in calm waters or on rubble to soft sandy to silt bottoms.

DEPTH RANGE: 2–12 m (6–40 ft). **DISTRIBUTION:** PNG, much of the Indo-Pacific. **IDEAL LENS:** 24–60 mm.

The green Halimeda Crab (*Huenia heraldica*) holds a piece of *Halimeda cylindracea* above its head like a set of antlers. Although the effect is to produce a different outline from when the crab is 'wearing' *H. macroloba* (see page 127), both 'headdresses' are confusing to a potential predator.
DEPTH RANGE: 2–12 m (6–40 ft). **DISTRIBUTION:** PNG, Australia. **IDEAL LENS:** 105 mm.

Using its prehensile tail to cling to a branch of coralline algae, the Dwarf Pipehorse (*Acentronura tentaculata*) is camouflaged by a covering of tufts. This pipehorse inhabits areas of low plant growth in coastal still-water bays.
DEPTH RANGE: 3–10 m (9–35 ft). **DISTRIBUTION:** PNG, Australia, Indonesia, Solomon Islands. **IDEAL LENS:** 105 mm.

Common in tropical waters, brown seaweeds of the genus *Sargassum* are often ripped from the bottom by strong wave action to float up onto the surface as large 'rafts' drifting with the current. The rafts often contain populations of small fish and other creatures well worth investigating, while larger pelagic fishes such as tuna congregate below.
DEPTH RANGE: 1–30 m (3–100 ft). **DISTRIBUTION:** PNG, much of the tropical Indo-Pacific. **IDEAL LENS:** 15 mm.

A frequent sailor on rafts of sargassum weed is the Sargassum Nudibranch (*Notobryon wardi*), which may be accompanied by a crew of various other creatures. Little is known about this nudibranch except that it feeds on hydroids and has its rhinophores supported on large stalks.

DEPTH RANGE: Surface. **DISTRIBUTION:** PNG, much of the Indo-Pacific. **IDEAL LENS:** 105 mm.

Adapted to a life on drifting rafts of sargassum weed, the Sargassum Anglerfish (*Histrio histrio*) matches the seaweed in both colour and shape. Its pale or dark brown body is covered in short leaf-like projections, enabling the fish to hide from predators. (The Sargassum Anglerfish is also pictured on page 121.)

DEPTH RANGE: Surface.

DISTRIBUTION: PNG, all tropical parts of the Indo-Pacific except the eastern Pacific.

IDEAL LENS: 60 mm.

Sea cucumbers belong to the same group as the sea stars and sea urchins and many of them play host to a variety of smaller creatures. The basic echinoderm body has been elongated and flopped on one side in the sea cucumber, its five-sided symmetry being manifest (though not always obviously) in the five rows of tube feet running the length of its body. Sea cucumbers are the vacuum cleaners of the ocean realm. Most crawl slowly over the sea floor taking in great quantities of sediment and detritus at one end, extracting the edible organic material and expelling the leftovers at the other, leaving a characteristic trail. Other species use their feeding tentacles to snare zooplankton from the current. The species pictured here, *Thelenota anax*, is found in almost any habitat with small amounts of sand. DEPTH RANGE: 5–40 m+ (15–125 ft+). DISTRIBUTION: PNG, throughout the Indo-Pacific. IDEAL LENS: 15–24 mm.

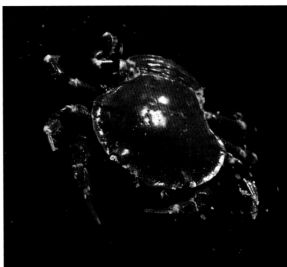

This inconspicuous swimmer crab, *Lissocarcinus orbicularis*, matches its host in colour and pattern. It is often found on the host's underside or lower edge, feeding on the sea floor.
DEPTH RANGE: 5–25 m (15–80 ft).
DISTRIBUTION: PNG, most of the Indo-Pacific.
IDEAL LENS: 60 mm.

Blushing a deep crimson will help this specimen of *Lissocarcinus orbicularis* hide on a black sea cucumber. Swimmer crabs characteristically have the last segment of the hind legs flattened to aid swimming and burrowing.
DEPTH RANGE: 5–25 m (15–80 ft).
DISTRIBUTION: PNG, most of the Indo-Pacific.
IDEAL LENS: 60 mm.

The perils of being a host: a large fish trying to feed on this *Lissocarcinus orbicularis* removed a large section from its host cucumber along with the crab. On tasting the cucumber the fish spat out the piece and the crab lived to see another day.
DEPTH RANGE: 5–25 m (15–80 ft).
DISTRIBUTION: PNG, most of the Indo-Pacific.
IDEAL LENS: 60 mm.

Inconspicuous on its host, the scale worm *Gastrolepidia clavigera* forages in among the soft lumpy skin of a number of sea cucumber species living in warm tropical waters. In each case it alters its colouration to match its living habitat.
DEPTH RANGE: 5–40 m+ (15–125 ft+).
DISTRIBUTION: PNG, much of the Indo-Pacific.
IDEAL LENS: 105 mm.

On the sandy weed and rubble zones around coral reefs many species of sea urchins cluster together, each with their entourage of hangers-on. Pictured here is the beautiful little Adam's Crab (*Zebrida adamsii*) which clings to a variety of sea urchins and feeds from the sea floor while remaining protected by the urchin's spines. (This crab is also pictured on page 111.)

DEPTH RANGE: 5–20 m (15–65 ft). **DISTRIBUTION:** PNG, the Indo-Pacific. **IDEAL LENS:** 60–105 mm.

A relatively long-spined species found on rubble slopes, the Radiant Sea Urchin (*Astropyga radiata*) has a bright red body with ten fluorescent blue dotted lines running from top to bottom; black to red spines cover the entire urchin.
DEPTH RANGE: 2–25 m (6–80 ft).
DISTRIBUTION: PNG, much of the Indo-Pacific.
IDEAL LENS: 24 mm.

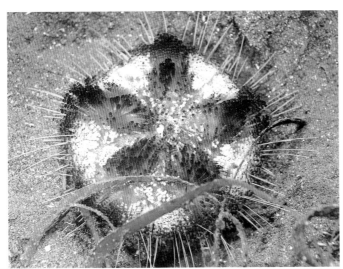

Hands off this urchin — its fluorescent-coloured spines are extremely painful to touch. When disturbed, the Fire Urchin (*Asthenosoma varium*) can move rapidly across the sea floor. (The Fire Urchin is also pictured on pages 110 and 111.)
DEPTH RANGE 5–40 m (15–125 ft).
DISTRIBUTION: PNG, Indonesia, most of the Indo-Pacific.
IDEAL LENS: 24 mm.

Looking here like a spiky lamington, the Cake Urchin (*Tripneustes gratilla*) can accessorise to suit the latest environmental trends. It is often found with pebbles, leaves or seaweed attached to itself. This is a common inhabitant of seagrass beds and rubble zones.
DEPTH RANGE 1–10 m (3–30 ft).
DISTRIBUTION: PNG, Indonesia, most of the Indo-Pacific.
IDEAL LENS: 60 mm.

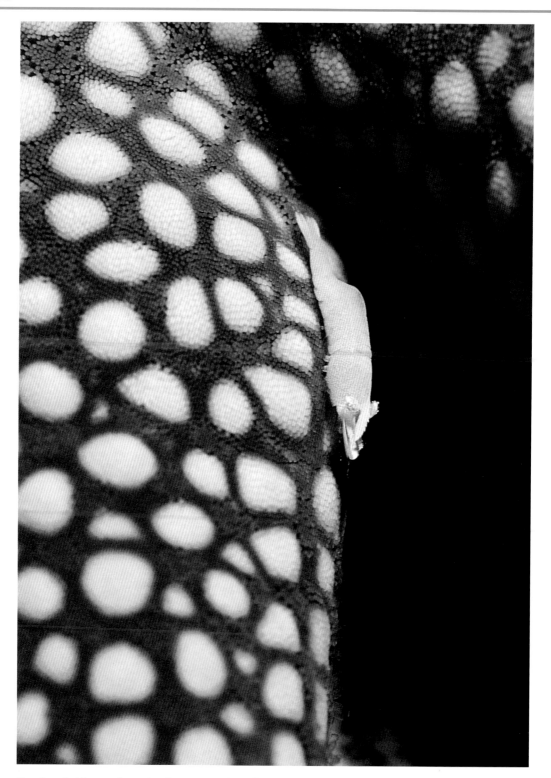

Sea stars stud the sea floors of reef areas everywhere. This species, *Nardoa novaecaledoniae*, is hosting the tiny Sea Star Shrimp (*Periclimenes soror*), a shrimp that inhabits a number of sea star species in a range of habitats, changing its colouring as it goes to blend in with its host.

DEPTH RANGE: 3–30 m+ (9–100 ft+). **DISTRIBUTION:** PNG, most of the Indo-Pacific. **IDEAL LENS:** 105 mm.

Looking like a yellow-speckled marshmallow, the sea star *Choriaster granulatus* is found both in sandy areas and on living reefs.
DEPTH RANGE: 4–40 m+ (12–125 ft+).
DISTRIBUTION: PNG, most of the Indo-Pacific.
IDEAL LENS: 24 mm.

Known as both the Chocolate-chip Sea Star and the Horned Sea Star, *Protoreaster nodosus* is found in shallow water on seagrass beds, often in large colonies.
DEPTH RANGE: 2–6 m (6–20 ft).
DISTRIBUTION: PNG, most of the Indo-Pacific.
IDEAL LENS: 24 mm.

A well-rounded sea star, the Cushion Star (*Culcita novaguineae*) is almost as thick as it is wide. It can be found in a variety of habitats but most often on sandy reef flats, feeding mainly on corals and other encrusting organisms. It may be yellow–green, brown or purple. Its gut is sometimes inhabited by a peculiar transparent fish.
DEPTH RANGE: 5–30 m (15–100 ft).
DISTRIBUTION: PNG, much of central Indo-Pacific.
IDEAL LENS: 15–24 mm.

This soft coral of the genus *Alertigorgia* grows in sandy silt areas in calm bays and hosts a variety of small creatures. Colonies of soft corals are attached to the sea bed and are supported internally by an arrangement of calcareous growths which give each species its own characteristic knobbly appearance.

DEPTH RANGE: 3–20 m (9–65 ft). DISTRIBUTION: PNG. IDEAL LENS: 24 mm.

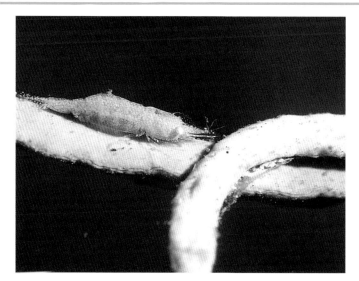

This very delicate-looking shrimp, a species of *Hamodactylus*, searches for food among the branches of an *Alertigorgia* soft coral.
DEPTH RANGE: 3–20 m (9–65 ft).
DISTRIBUTION: PNG.
IDEAL LENS: 105 mm.

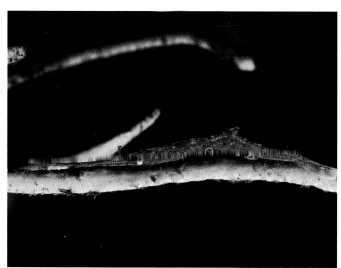

The Longnose Shrimp (*Tozeuma armatum)* is found on a variety of soft corals, including species of *Alertigorgia*. Its elongated body makes it inconspicuous.
DEPTH RANGE: 6–40 m (20–125 ft).
DISTRIBUTION: PNG.
IDEAL LENS: 105 mm.

The spindle-shaped allied cowry *Hiatovula brunneiterma* has brown tips and a white mantle with dark spots, and is hosted by an *Alertigorgia* species of soft coral. Spindle cowries are generally well camouflaged and differ from true cowries in that they lack teeth on their aperture.
DEPTH RANGE: 3–20 m (9–65 ft).
DISTRIBUTION: PNG, Australia, Philippines, Solomon Islands.
IDEAL LENS: 105 mm.

The elegantly structured Chambered Nautilus (*Nautilus pompilius*) can usually be found on the sea floor at depths of 150 m+ (490 ft+), chasing crabs among coral rubble. At night it swims into shallower waters, rising to prey upon small fish. *Nautilus* use their strong sense of smell to track their prey and, because of their ability to adjust the distribution of gas within each chamber, are deft at moving through the water column.
DEPTH RANGE: 200–300 m (600–1000 ft). **DISTRIBUTION:** PNG, central Indo-Pacific. **IDEAL LENS:** 24–60 mm.

A slithering suite of Banded Sea Snakes? No — just a Mimic Octopus (*Octopus* sp.) living up to its name. This octopus can be found in sandy pebble bottoms and sandy grass areas, mimicking the Banded Sea Snake and various species of flounder, sole, mantis shrimp and bottom-dwelling sting ray.

DEPTH RANGE: 3–30 m (9–100 ft).

DISTRIBUTION: PNG, Indonesia.

IDEAL LENS: 24–60 mm.

More delicately striped than the Mimic Octopus, the beautiful Ornate Octopus (*Octopus* sp.) has been observed trying to mimic such creatures as sea snakes and lionfish.

DEPTH RANGE: 3–30 m (9–100 ft).

DISTRIBUTION: PNG, Indonesia.

IDEAL LENS: 60 mm.

This small unidentified octopus was seen moving along a soft sandy bottom on Observation Point, Milne Bay in Papua New Guinea. As it moved along the bottom, it rapidly changed its colouration to match its background. This photograph was taken at one of the few moments when it was clearly visible.

DEPTH RANGE: 3 m (9 ft)

DISTRIBUTION: PNG.

IDEAL LENS: 105 mm.

Looking like it's spent too long in the sun, *Octopus luteus* is almost entirely red–brown in colour with white freckles; even its eyes are red. This octopus is active at night hunting among stony rubble and sand areas.
DEPTH RANGE: 2–30 m (6–100 ft).
DISTRIBUTION: PNG, Australia, New Zealand, Indonesia, Philippines, Taiwan.
IDEAL LENS: 24 mm.

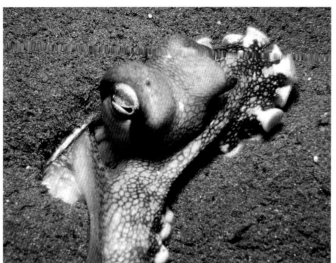

Startled, this unidentified octopus began retreating into the sand as soon as the photographer approached. It eventually disappeared completely.
DEPTH RANGE: 6 m (20 ft).
DISTRIBUTION: PNG.
IDEAL LENS: 60 mm.

This very shy octopus was quick to bury itself when faced with oncoming divers. Octopuses are by nature shy and shun publicity, so some stealth is required if you want to photograph them complete.
DEPTH RANGE: 2 m (6 ft).
DISTRIBUTION: PNG.
IDEAL LENS: 60 mm.

This red octopus is similar to *Octopus luteus* but lacks its characteristic white spots. It is active only at night and is seen here with its eyes closed due to the diver's light.
DEPTH RANGE: 6 m (20 ft).
DISTRIBUTION: PNG.
IDEAL LENS: 24–60 mm.

This small species of hairy octopus was only recently discovered on a night dive in Milne Bay, Papua New Guinea by the author. At this stage very little is known about it, other than that it prefers areas where there is a lot of debris.
DEPTH RANGE: 20 m (65 ft).
DISTRIBUTION: PNG.
IDEAL LENS: 60 mm.

The gregarious Reef Octopus (*Octopus cyanea*) can often be found in large groups. It is seen on live reefs in many locations, and on rubble bottoms, where it makes its den. Females of this species lay a mass of tiny capsule-shaped eggs and sit over them for some 5–6 weeks, until they hatch.
DEPTH RANGE: 3–40 m (9–125 ft).
DISTRIBUTION: PNG, throughout the Pacific.
IDEAL LENS: 24–60 mm.

The elusive Pfeffer's Flamboyant Cuttlefish (*Metasepia pfefferi*) is much sought-after by photographers. A good place to search for it is on sandy bottoms or slopes.
DEPTH RANGE: 3–40 m+ (9–125 ft+).
DISTRIBUTION: PNG, Australia, Indonesia.
IDEAL LENS: 60–105 mm.

Confusingly this, too, is a Pfeffer's Flamboyant Cuttlefish. It has changed its colour to suit the debris among which it was found. It is best recognised by its squat little body and flattened 'arms'. (This cuttlefish is also pictured on page 171.)
DEPTH RANGE: 3–40 m+ (9–125 ft+).
DISTRIBUTION: PNG, Australia, Indonesia.
IDEAL LENS: 60–105 mm.

Dumpling or bobtail squid from the genus *Eupyrmna* like burrowing into soft sandy silt to hide by day. At night they employ luminescent bacteria in their body to confuse predators. (This squid is also pictured on page 162.)
DEPTH RANGE: 2–30 m (6–100 ft).
DISTRIBUTION: PNG, Australia, much of central Indo-Pacific.
IDEAL LENS: 105 mm.

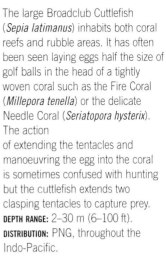

The large Broadclub Cuttlefish (*Sepia latimanus*) inhabits both coral reefs and rubble areas. It has often been seen laying eggs half the size of golf balls in the head of a tightly woven coral such as the Fire Coral (*Millepora tenella*) or the delicate Needle Coral (*Seriatopora hysterix*). The action of extending the tentacles and manoeuvring the egg into the coral is sometimes confused with hunting but the cuttlefish extends two clasping tentacles to capture prey.
DEPTH RANGE: 2–30 m (6–100 ft).
DISTRIBUTION: PNG, throughout the Indo-Pacific.
IDEAL LENS: 60 mm.

At no bigger than two matchstick heads, this tiny creature is possibly a juvenile bobtail squid (*Eupyrma* sp.)
DEPTH RANGE: 4 m (12 ft).
DISTRIBUTION: PNG.
IDEAL LENS: 105 mm.

Blushing in response to being startled, this small cuttlefish, a species of *Sepia*, is usually extremely hard to spot among the coralline alga *Halimeda macroloba*. Just over 30 mm (¼ in) long, it was photographed in 40 m (125 ft) of water.
DEPTH RANGE: 20–40 m (65–125 ft).
DISTRIBUTION: PNG.
IDEAL LENS: 105 mm.

It is unusual to find a stargazer above the sand, as they usually bury themselves with only their dorsally mounted eyes clear of the surface. Do not touch this fish as it has extremely sharp spines behind its pectoral fins.
DEPTH RANGE: 1–30 m (3–100 ft).
DISTRIBUTION: PNG, Indonesia, Australia.
IDEAL LENS: 20–60 mm.

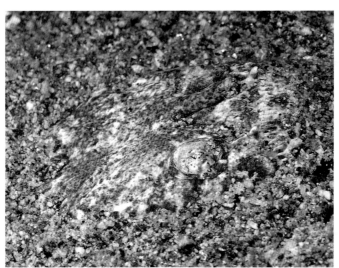

A protruding, wiggling lure may be the only sign that a hungry Marbled Stargazer (*Uranoscopus bicinctus*) lurks within the sandy substrate. With its eyes just exposed, the stargazer takes advantage of curious fish and cephalopods by quickly protruding its mouth and sucking in whole prey.
DEPTH RANGE: 1–30 m (3–100 ft).
DISTRIBUTION: PNG, Indonesia, Australia.
IDEAL LENS: 20–60 mm.

Another inhabitant of sandy bottoms is the marvellously camouflaged Leopard Flounder (*Bothus pantherinus*). Only its protruding eyes give it away, and they are not easy to spot!
DEPTH RANGE: 1–20 m (3–65 ft).
DISTRIBUTION: PNG, Indonesia, Australia, Solomon Islands, Philippines.
IDEAL LENS: 60 mm.

The torpedo-shaped Snake Fish (*Trachinocephalus myops*) buries itself in soft sand when disturbed, leaving only its eyes and mouth exposed. When out in the open it can be easily identified by the blue lines along its body. Small, scattered groups of these fish usually share the same habitat, preferring slopes and open sandy areas in coastal bays and estuaries.
DEPTH RANGE: 2–40 m (6–125 ft).
DISTRIBUTION: PNG, much of the Indo-Pacific.
IDEAL LENS: 105 mm.

This small juvenile Starry Toadfish (*Arothron stellatus*) was found investigating a rubble area. Juveniles prefer muddy areas with debris on shallow coastal slopes. As the fish grows its stripes will break up into spots.
DEPTH RANGE: 3 m (9 ft).
DISTRIBUTION: PNG.
IDEAL LENS: 105 mm.

The spots of this adult Starry Toadfish have replaced its juvenile stripes. Once this transformation has taken place adults move to sandy slopes and rubble bottoms close to main reef patches.
DEPTH RANGE: 3–30 m (9–100 ft).
DISTRIBUTION: PNG, much of the Indo-Pacific.
IDEAL LENS: 60 mm.

Bolting along like a sea floor hovercraft, this flathead may be moving in on a meal. Flatheads wait on the seabed to ambush passing fish, crustaceans or cephalopods. Identification of flathead to the species level depends often only on the spiny features on their head.
DEPTH RANGE: 3–20 m (9–65 ft).
DISTRIBUTION: PNG, much of the central Indo-Pacific.
IDEAL LENS: 60 mm.

Skulking in the sediment of the sea floor, this flathead is barely visible. Although impossible to identify, this photograph illustrates just one of the brilliant strategies employed by marine creatures and emphasises how careful examination around reefs will reveal so much more.
DEPTH RANGE: 3–20 m (9–65 ft).
DISTRIBUTION: PNG, much of the central Indo-Pacific.
IDEAL LENS: 60 mm.

Slender and eel-like, the Spotted Sand-diver (*Trichonotus setiger*) inhabits soft sand slopes, 'diving' below the sand when it feels threatened. It feeds on juvenile fish and small invertebrates. Sand-divers are often seen in large schools hovering just above the sand, ready to dash for cover at the slightest disturbance.
DEPTH RANGE: 2–25 m (6–80 ft).
DISTRIBUTION: PNG.
IDEAL LENS: 105 mm.

The Banded Sole (*Soleichthys hcterohinos*) is often found lying on rocks during the night. During the day it prefers sandy bottoms, only the snorkel and eyes being visible. The snorkel allows the sole to breathe underground.
DEPTH RANGE: 2–10 m (6–35 ft). **DISTRIBUTION:** PNG. **IDEAL LENS:** 60 mm.

A closeup of the Banded Sole showing only eyes and snorkel above the sea bed.
DEPTH RANGE: 2–10 m (6–35 ft). **DISTRIBUTION:** PNG. **IDEAL LENS:** 60 mm.

Highly variable in colour and pattern, the Ornate Ghost Pipefish (*Solenostomus paradoxus*), like other species of this genus, often mimics invertebrates, algae or weeds, thereby remaining undetected.
DEPTH RANGE: 5–40 m+ (15–125 ft+).
DISTRIBUTION: PNG, Solomon Islands, Australia, Indonesia.
IDEAL LENS: 60–105 mm.

Here is another colour variation of the Ornate Ghost Pipefish. Commonly inhabiting still bays in or around seagrass beds, often in association with black coral or feather stars, it is also seen on drop-offs and coral reefs.
DEPTH RANGE: 5–40 m+ (15–125 ft+)
DISTRIBUTION: PNG, Solomon Islands, Australia, Indonesia.
IDEAL LENS: 60–105 mm.

This adult Ornate Ghost Pipefish is in yet another guise.
DEPTH RANGE: 5–40 m+ (15–125 ft+).
DISTRIBUTION: PNG, Solomon Islands, Australia, Indonesia.
IDEAL LENS: 60–105 mm.

This little Ornate Ghost Pipefish is a juvenile.
DEPTH RANGE: 5–40 m+ (15–125 ft+).
DISTRIBUTION: PNG, Solomon Islands, Australia, Indonesia.
IDEAL LENS: 60–105 mm.

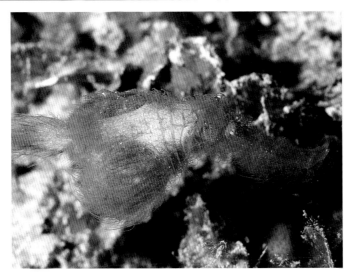

The shy Hairy Ghost Pipefish (*Solenostomus* sp.) can usually be found on rocky slopes where red algae grow. (This pipefish is also pictured on page 165.)
DEPTH RANGE: 5–30 m (15–100 ft).
DISTRIBUTION: PNG, Solomon Islands, Indonesia, northern Australia.
IDEAL LENS: 105 mm.

Another creature that avoids the limelight, the Robust Ghost Pipefish (*Solenostomus cyanopterus*) is coloured and patterned to blend in with its environment. Found in the seagrass beds of quiet bays, it alters its appearance as the grasses or algae it mimics mature and change in texture and colour.
DEPTH RANGE: 1–10 m (3–35 ft).
DISTRIBUTION: PNG, Australia, Solomon Islands, Indonesia.
IDEAL LENS: 60 mm.

This is just another colour variation of the Robust Ghost Pipefish. The species is generally found in shallow waters where the sand meets the grass beds and debris tends to accumulate.
DEPTH RANGE: 0–10 m (0–35 ft).
DISTRIBUTION: PNG, Australia, Solomon Islands, throughout the Indo-Pacific.
IDEAL LENS: 105 mm.

Found among the coralline alga *Halimeda macroloba*, usually on sandy rubble bottoms, is the Long-tail Ghost Pipefish (*Solenostomus armatus*), whose fins take on the general shape of the weed's branches.
DEPTH RANGE: 1–10 m (3–35 ft).
DISTRIBUTION: PNG, Solomon Islands, Indonesia, Philippines, northern Australia.
IDEAL LENS: 105 mm.

Hovering close to swaying weed is another colour variation of the Long-tail Ghost Pipefish. The weed provides rich feeding grounds as well as camouflage.
DEPTH RANGE: 1–10 m (3–35 ft).
DISTRIBUTION: PNG, Solomon Islands, Indonesia, Philippines, northern Australia.
IDEAL LENS: 105 mm.

There are two Long-tail Ghost Pipefish in this picture. The smaller one on the right is the male. The female carries eggs in a 'pouch' on her underside.
DEPTH RANGE: 1–10 m (3–35 ft).
DISTRIBUTION: PNG, Solomon Islands, Indonesia, Philippines, northern Australia.
IDEAL LENS: 105 mm.

The Banded Pipefish (*Doryrhamphus dactyliophurus*) is often found under old piers, in and around wrecks, or with long-spined urchins or corals protruding from a sandy silt bottom. Males carry the eggs attached to their body.
DEPTH RANGE: 5–30 m (15–100 ft). DISTRIBUTION: PNG, much of the Indo-Pacific. IDEAL LENS: 24–60 mm.

The Double-ended Pipehorse (*Syngnathoides biaculeatus*) is often mistaken for a strand of seaweed. Not surprisingly, it inhabits seagrass beds and can often be found in large rafts of sargassum weed.
DEPTH RANGE: 1–10 m (3–35 ft). DISTRIBUTION: PNG, Solomon Islands, Indonesia, Australia. IDEAL LENS: 60 mm.

Groups of the Messmate Pipefish (*Corythoichthys intestinalis*) inhabit sandy slopes near reefs, or on reef tops where sand gathers. They are also very common in the sand and rubble around jetties.
DEPTH RANGE: 2–10 m (6–35 ft).
DISTRIBUTION: PNG, Australia, Indonesia, Solomon Islands.
IDEAL LENS: 60 mm.

Inhabiting sandy rubble areas and sand patches near, or on top of, reefs or wrecks, Schultz's Pipefish (*Corythoichthys schultzi*) is coloured and patterned to blend with its surroundings. Its longer snout and regularly-spaced alternating dark and light lines distinguish it from the similar-looking Reeftop Pipefish (*C. haematopterus*).
DEPTH RANGE: 2–10 m (6–35 ft).
DISTRIBUTION: PNG, Australia, Solomon Islands.
IDEAL LENS: 60 mm.

The large Winged Pipefish (*Halicampus macrorhynchus*) can be found on rubble bottoms, drop-offs and reef slopes. It is distinguished by the series of 'wings' on its back.
DEPTH RANGE: 3–20 m (9–65 ft).
DISTRIBUTION: PNG, Australia, Indonesia.
IDEAL LENS: 60–24 mm.

The recently described Randall's Shrimp Goby (*Amblyeleotris randalli*) lives in sandy areas on or around reefs. Like the Bumble-bee Goby (right), it guards the burrow it shares with the blind shrimp, *Alpheus ranalli.*
DEPTH RANGE: 5–20 m (15–65 ft).
DISTRIBUTION: PNG, Australia, Indonesia, Solomon Islands.
IDEAL LENS: 105 mm.

You will find the strikingly-coloured Bumble-bee Goby (*Stonogobiops xanthorhinica*) in sandy rubble areas close to its burrow, which it shares in a symbiotic relationship with the blind shrimp, *Alpheus ranalli.*
DEPTH RANGE: 10–25 m (35–80 ft).
DISTRIBUTION: PNG.
IDEAL LENS: 105 mm.

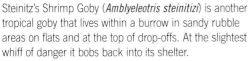

Steinitz's Shrimp Goby (*Amblyeleotris steinitzi*) is another tropical goby that lives within a burrow in sandy rubble areas on flats and at the top of drop-offs. At the slightest whiff of danger it bobs back into its shelter.
DEPTH RANGE: 3–25 m (9–80 ft).
DISTRIBUTION: PNG, throughout the Indo-Pacific.
IDEAL LENS: 105 mm.

When startled the Twin-spot or Crab-eyed Goby (*Signigobius biocellatus*) raises its dorsal fins to simulate a sideways-moving crab. It lives in sandy areas of the reef, typically at the bases of cliffs and bommies.
DEPTH RANGE: 5–25 m (15–80 ft).
DISTRIBUTION: PNG, Solomon Islands, Australia, Indonesia.
IDEAL LENS: 105 mm.

This Crested Sabretooth Blenny (*Petroscirtes mitratus*) is among the coralline algae *Halimeda macroloba* on a sandy rubble bottom. Adults have also been seen on jetty pylons and juveniles may float with sargassum weed.
DEPTH RANGE: 2 m (6 ft).
DISTRIBUTION: PNG. **IDEAL LENS:** 105 mm.

The Banded Blenny (*Salarias fasciatus*) is inconspicuous when settled on algae in rubble areas. It is also observed close to wharf sites and among corals in still waters.
DEPTH RANGE: 1–10 m (3–35 ft).
DISTRIBUTION: PNG, throughout the Indo-Pacific.
IDEAL LENS: 105 mm.

This white-faced waspfish from the genus *Richardsonichthys* lies buried in sandy silt all day but emerges at night to feed on small shrimps and crustaceans.
DEPTH RANGE: 3–30 m (9–100 ft).
DISTRIBUTION: PNG, Indonesia, Japan.
IDEAL LENS: 60 mm.

More often found in rubble areas (as shown on page 86), this False Stonefish (*Scorpaenopsis diabolus*) was found in a seagrass area close to an estuary.
DEPTH RANGE: 1–15 m (3–50 ft).
DISTRIBUTION: PNG, most of the Indo-Pacific.
IDEAL LENS: 60 mm.

Despite its show-off colours, the Mandarinfish (*Synchiropus splendidus*) is very shy. Whole families often take up residence in the polyps of a densely-branching coral, dominated by a brightly-coloured male. Such corals occupy areas rich in algae in quiet, shallow waters.
DEPTH RANGE: 2–9 m (6–35 ft).
DISTRIBUTION: PNG, Australia, Indonesia, most of the western Pacific.
IDEAL LENS: 105 mm.

A flighty fish, the Flying Gurnard (*Dactyloptena orientalis*) is easily disturbed, startling predators with a display of its wings before taking off with a burst of speed. Usually partly buried in the sea floor, it sometimes rises to be found on sandy slopes.
DEPTH RANGE: 2–40 m+ (6–125 ft+).
DISTRIBUTION: PNG, much of the Indo-Pacific.
IDEAL LENS: 105 mm.

Showing its distinct juvenile colouration, this young Flying Gurnard was found in shallow water. Juveniles usually inhabit the sandy seaweed slopes that drop off into deep water.
DEPTH RANGE: 3–40 m+ (9–125 ft+).
DISTRIBUTION: PNG, Australia, Indonesia, Solomon Islands.
IDEAL LENS: 105 mm.

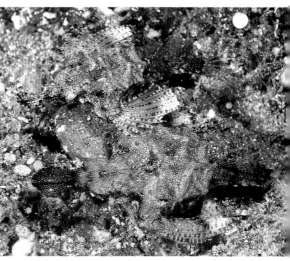

By night, the small Blue-eyed Stingfish (*Minous trachy-cephalus*) moves along the sea floor in search of food and remains buried in the sand by day. Its eyes glow a royal blue when they catch the light. (This fish is also pictured on page 91.)
DEPTH RANGE: 3–30 m (9–100 ft).
DISTRIBUTION: PNG, Indonesia, Japan.
IDEAL LENS: 60 mm.

Able to mimic shell fragments and small stones, Little Dragonfish (*Eurypegasus dragonis*) can be very difficult to find. Usually in pairs, they 'walk' along on their leg-like pectoral fins. Male pectoral fins have a broad blue–white margin used in display and to startle predators.
DEPTH RANGE: 3–25 m (9–80 ft).
DISTRIBUTION: PNG, Indonesia, Australia.
IDEAL LENS: 60 mm.

Highly photogenic, the Common Seahorse (*Hippocampus kuda*) may be black, brown or yellow and shades in between, sometimes with minute black spots. Adults are mainly found in seagrasses in shallow-water estuaries and bays with rubble bottoms, usually in pairs. Occasionally an adult is found attached to a piece of weed a long way from its usual habitat. Juveniles, too, often attach themselves to floating weeds.
DEPTH RANGE: 1–20 m (3–65 ft).
DISTRIBUTION: PNG, much of the Indo-Pacific.
IDEAL LENS: 60 mm.

Like all seahorses, the Common Seahorse has a prehensile tail which it is able to wind tightly around living holdfasts to secure it in a strong current.
DEPTH RANGE: 1–20 m (3–65 ft).
DISTRIBUTION: PNG, much of the Indo-Pacific.
IDEAL LENS: 60 mm.

This is yet a third colour variation of the Common Seahorse. These colour changes are a response to the changing colours of the seahorse's habitat as it swims or floats around.
DEPTH RANGE: 1–20 m (3–65 ft).
DISTRIBUTION: PNG, much of the Indo-Pacific.
IDEAL LENS: 60 mm.

Filefish of the genus *Acreichthys* live and feed in long seagrasses and in seaweed beds, adopting the colour of their habitat.

DEPTH RANGE: 1–10 m (3–35 ft).
DISTRIBUTION: PNG, Solomon Islands, most of the Indo-Pacific.
IDEAL LENS: 105 mm.

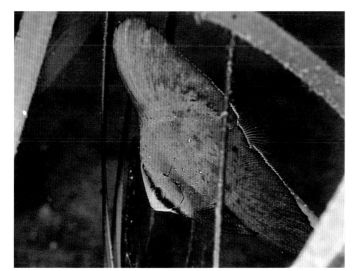

A juvenile Round Batfish (*Platax orbicularis*) photographed among tall seagrass. Young batfish often float in rafts of sargassum weed. When sensing a potential predator approaching from below, they flatten themselves against whatever surface they can find in order to be less conspicuous.

DEPTH RANGE: 2 m (6 ft).
DISTRIBUTION: PNG, most of the Indo-Pacific.
IDEAL LENS: 60 mm.

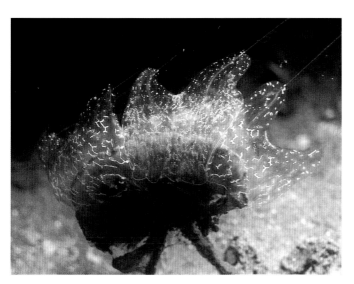

Despite their delicate appearance — or perhaps in keeping with their ghoulish glow — comb jellies are fierce predators, fond of devouring small fish and even other comb jellies. Often mistaken for jellyfish, comb jellies are classified in a group of their own. Pictured here, the comb jelly *Coeloplana meteoris* inhabits soft silty bottoms. Sitting on anything that raises them above the sea floor, they stretch out branching tentacles and pull in passing plankton.

DEPTH RANGE: 3–40 m (9–125 ft).
DISTRIBUTION: PNG, Australia, Indonesia.
IDEAL LENS: 60 mm.

CHAPTER 7
PHOTOGRAPHING THE CREATURES

Producing good photographs of undersea creatures requires a range of techniques. Position your subject so that it lies between your camera lens and the open water, and ensure that there is nothing in the subject's background that will reflect light back to your camera. Once you have found a suitable position, aim one or more strobes at the subject and photograph it using a high f-stop. This will give your subject a black background and only the light reflected off your subject will be captured on the film. The high f-stop will slightly increase your depth of field, thereby producing a sharper image. I believe photographs produced this way have a greater impact, the colours and lines being strongly pronounced against a clear background.

In addition, slow film produces intense colours because of a reduction in grain size. Remember that the slower the film the more light is needed for proper exposure. This can be achieved using a stronger strobe or by letting more light into your camera by lowering the f-stop.

In macrophotography both single and dual strobes are used. Although a single strobe casts shadows, you can adjust the strobe's angle. Dual strobes will generally eliminate shadows.

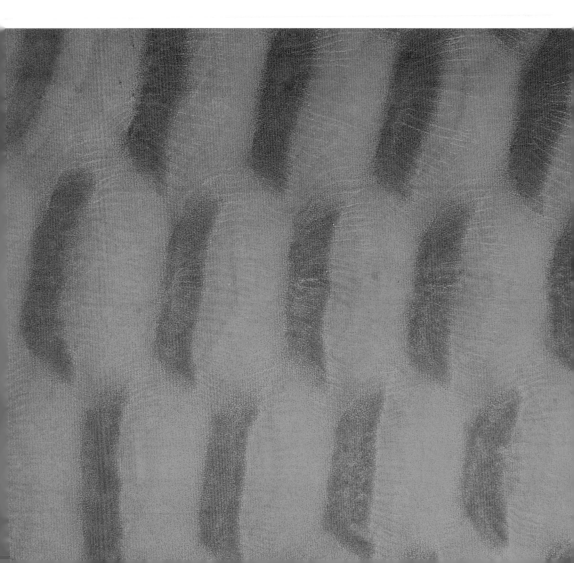

Here Bleeker's Parrotfish, like many species of parrotfish, has secreted a mucous cocoon around its body to trap its body odour, thereby avoiding detection by night predators. This photograph was taken at f/22 for 1/60 second using 50 ASA film.
DEPTH RANGE: 5 m (15 ft).
DISTRIBUTION: PNG.
IDEAL LENS: 60 mm.

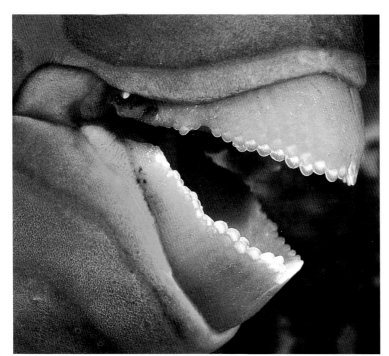

Parrotfish have very strong teeth with which they rasp away food from hard surfaces on the reef. This close-up photograph of the Two-colour Parrotfish (*Cetoscarus bicolour*), taken at f/22 for 1/60 second using 50 ASA film, shows the wear and tear on its teeth.
DEPTH RANGE: 15 m (45 ft).
DISTRIBUTION: PNG, much of the Indo-Pacific.
IDEAL LENS: 105 mm.

OPPOSITE: Like the scales of many fish, those of Bleeker's Parrotfish (*Scarus bleekeri*) make attractive pictures when photographed using a macro lens and blown up to poster size. This close-up photograph was taken at f/22 for 1/60 second using 50 ASA film.
DEPTH RANGE: 15 m (45 ft). **DISTRIBUTION:** PNG, much of the Indo-Pacific. **IDEAL LENS:** 105 mm.

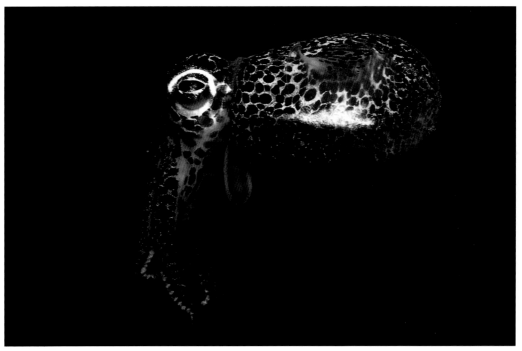

This curious, shy creature is a dumpling or bobtail squid from the genus *Eupyrmna*. Usually buried in sand or silt by day (top) it emerges from its daytime slumber to take position on the sea floor and wait for prey. This photograph was taken at f/22 for 1/60 second using 50 ASA film. The squid above, taken at f/22 for 1/60 second using 64 ASA film, seems dazed by the camera's light as it ventures from the bottom. Against the dark water, the fluorescent body colours and patterns are far more apparent. (This squid is also pictured on page 144.)

DEPTH RANGE: 5–30+ m (15–100+ ft). DISTRIBUTION: PNG, Indonesia, Australia. IDEAL LENS: 105 mm.

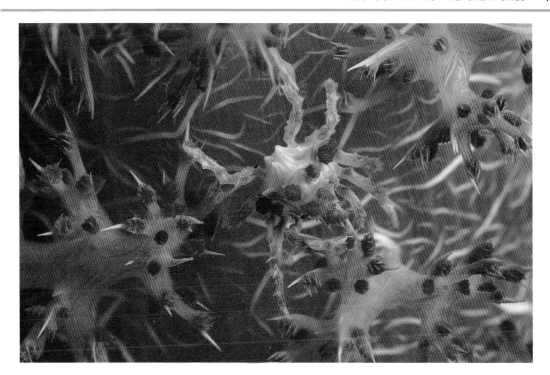

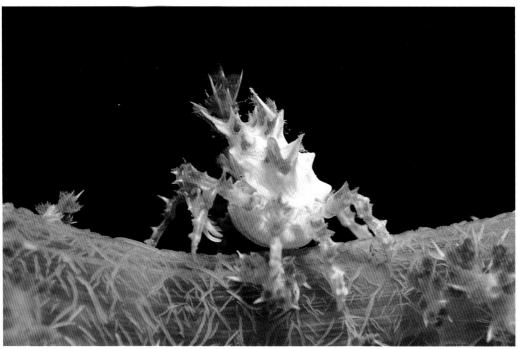

The Dendronephthya Crab (*Hoplophrys oatesii*) lives among the spines of soft corals of the genus *Dendronephthya*. Although the top photograph illustrates how magnificently these crabs blend with their habitat, the lower one, shot against a backdrop of dark water reveals the exquisite structure of this animal. With macrophotography try to fill the frame with your subject, shooting at a low angle from either head-on or slightly to one side. Both of these photographs were taken at f/22 for 1/60 second using 50 ASA film. (This crab is also pictured on page 15.)
DEPTH RANGE: 5–30 m (15–100 ft). **DISTRIBUTION:** PNG, much of Indo-Pacific. **IDEAL LENS:** 105 mm.

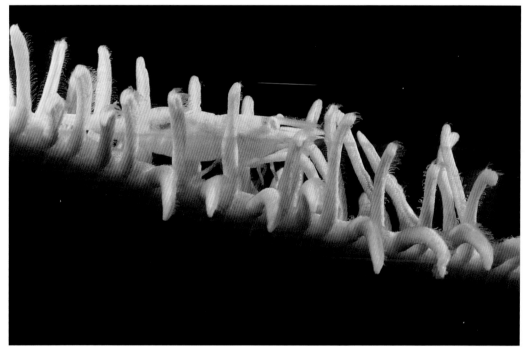

Photographing the crinoid shrimp *Periclimenes amboinensis* in the arms of its feather star host was an exercise of patience, waiting for the shrimp to move from the host's centre and along one of its arms. Avoid touching the feather star as it will close up around the shrimp in response. Adopting the colour of its host, the shrimp can be difficult to discern against a busy background (top) or even a not-so-busy background (above). Both photographs were taken at f/22 for 1/60 second using 50 ASA film. (This shrimp is also pictured on page 11.)

DEPTH RANGE: 5–20 m (15–65 ft). **DISTRIBUTION:** PNG, Indonesia, Solomon Islands, Australia. **IDEAL LENS:** 105 mm.

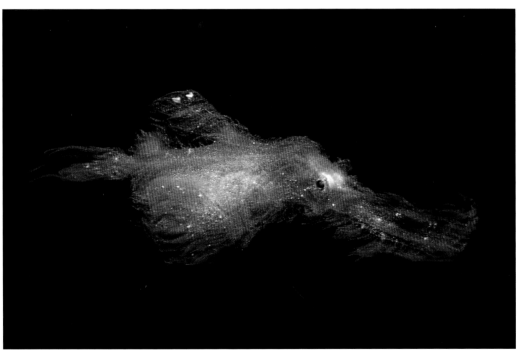

The detail of the extraordinary Hairy Ghost Pipefish (*Solenostomus* sp.), much sought-after by photographers, is better displayed against a plain background. The 'hair' of this pipefish, once thought to be a covering of red algae that had attached itself to the fish, is now known to be tissue produced by the fish as a form of camouflage, allowing it to hide in areas of red algae. The top photograph was taken at f/16 for 1/60 second using 50 ASA film and the one above was taken at f/22 for 1/60 second using 64 ASA film. (This pipefish is also pictured on page 151.)

DEPTH RANGE: 5–30 m (15–100 ft). **DISTRIBUTION:** PNG, Solomon Islands, Australia, Indonesia. **IDEAL LENS:** 105 mm.

While both images of the nudibranch *Gymnodoris ceylonica* are compelling, they impart different information. The top photo shows the nudibranch in its habitat and attended by a commensal shrimp. This was taken with one strobe placed slightly behind the other to create a slight shadow beneath the nudibranch, and at f/16 for 1/60 second using 50 ASA film. The other photo, shot with one strobe at 10 o'clock and the other at 2 o'clock to saturate the subject with light, was set to f/22 for 1/60 second, and 64 ASA film. (This nudibranch also appears on page 55.)
DEPTH RANGE: 3–30 m (9–100 ft). **DISTRIBUTION:** PNG, much of the Indo-Pacific. **IDEAL LENS:** 60 mm.

When photographing moving subjects such as the Reef Squid (*Sepioteuthis lessoniana*) pictured here, use a fast shutter speed to maintain the image's clarity. Even in the daytime (top) squid shimmer but it is at night that they really put on the most impressive influorescent light shows (above). This squid is mostly found in the water column where it feeds on small fish but it also appears on open reefs and in coastal bays and mangrove areas. Both photographs were taken at f/22 for 1/60 second using 50 ASA film.

DEPTH RANGE: 0–10 m (35 ft). **DISTRIBUTION:** PNG, throughout the Indo-Pacific. **IDEAL LENS:** 60–105 mm.

The Zebra Lionfish (*Dendrochirus zebra*) prefers rubble to sandy silt bottoms, seeking out rocks or logs which make a less than ideal background for photographs (top). The top photograph was taken at f/16 whereas the one immediately above was taken at f/22, both for 1/60 second using 50 ASA film. When photographing any creature, try to get as much of the subject as possible into focus; at the very least the eyes — or in the case of nudibranchs, the rhinophores — should be in focus. (This lionfish is also pictured on page 84.)

DEPTH RANGE: 3–40 m+ (9–125 ft+). **DISTRIBUTION:** PNG, much of the Indo-Pacific. **IDEAL LENS:** 60 mm.

The beautiful Christmas-tree Worm (*Spirobranchus giganteus*) comes in an assortment of colours — yellows, reds, blues, oranges and most colours in between. These colours can be hard to appreciate against the busy background of the worm's living coral host (top) but in the photograph immediately above, where there is no distracting background, the subject has a greater impact because it focuses the eye directly upon it. Both photographs on this page were taken at f/22 for 1/60 second using 50 ASA film. (This worm is also pictured on pages 31 and 119.)
DEPTH RANGE: 3–10 m (9–35 ft). **DISTRIBUTION:** PNG, much of the Indo-Pacific. **IDEAL LENS:** 105 mm.

Porcupinefish 'inflate' themselves by sucking in water, thereby appearing more of a challenge to potential predators. The top photograph, which shows a Rounded Porcupinefish (*Cyclichthys orbicularis*) that has wedged itself into a crevice on the sea floor at 40 m (132 ft) for protection, was taken at f/16 for 1/60 second using 50 ASA film. The photograph above of the Blotched Porcupinefish (*Dicotylichthys punctulatus*) was taken in the water column at f/16 for 1/60 second using 64 ASA film. Note that even though only part of the fish is visible, the image is still engaging as the focus is centred on the animal's eye.

DEPTH RANGE: 5–40 m (15–125 ft). **DISTRIBUTION:** PNG, throughout Indo-Pacific. **IDEAL LENS:** 20-24 mm.

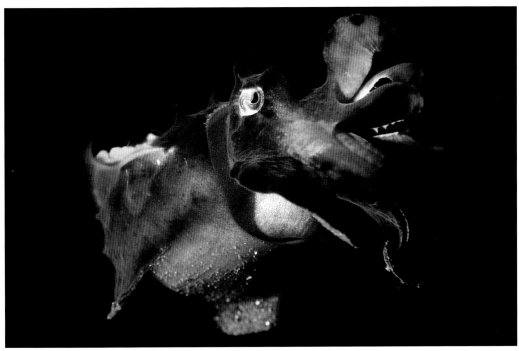

Pfeffer's Flamboyant Cuttlefish (*Metasepia pfefferi*) is very shy. Usually found in a sandy silt habitat, often in association with debris, it rarely moves far into the water column. It is, however, a very popular subject with photographers because of its ability to change colours and shots are most spectacular when the subject is set against a plain dark sea. If you find this cuttlefish in the water column, position your camera low to the ground and shoot upwards. Both the above photographs were taken at night at f/16 for 1/60 second using 50 ASA film. (This cuttlefish is also pictured on page 144.)

DEPTH RANGE: 3–40 m+ (9–125 ft+). **DISTRIBUTION:** PNG, Australia, Indonesia. **IDEAL LENS:** 60–105 mm.

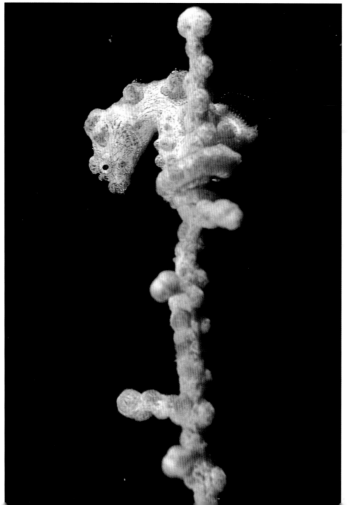

As the upper photograph shows, the Pygmy Seahorse (*Hippocampus bargibanti*) is very difficult to photograph clearly on its host sea fan, a species of *Muricella*, as it matches almost perfectly in bumps and colour. However, the creature is much easier to discern when photographed against a black background, as in the lower picture. Both photographs were taken at f/22 for 1/60 second using 50 ASA film. (This seahorse is also pictured on page 39.)

DEPTH RANGE: 15–50 m (50–165 ft).

DISTRIBUTION: PNG, Indonesia, Australia.

IDEAL LENS: 105 mm with + 2 dioptre.

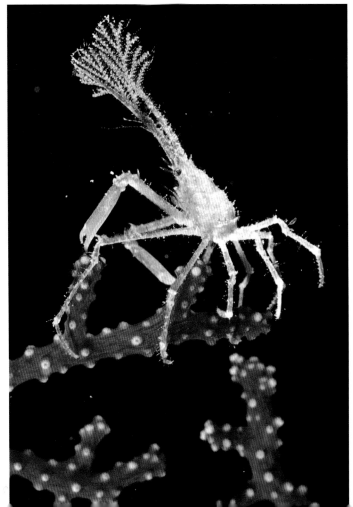

The oddly-shaped decorator crab, *Hyastenus dispinosus*, matches itself so closely to its host sea fans and soft corals that it can only be truly appreciated against a plain background. To avoid highlighting particles suspended in the water column (called 'backscatter'), angle your strobes from the sides and minimise the distance between you and your subject. Both photographs were taken at f/22 for 1/60 second using 50 ASA film.

DEPTH RANGE: 3–25 m (9–80 ft).
DISTRIBUTION: PNG, much of the central Indo-Pacific.
IDEAL LENS: 105 mm.

COMMON NAMES INDEX

LATIN NAMES INDEX